There is no joy and no service that can match helping others. In a world so full of darkness, where millions have lost their way, where there are countless numbers troubled and perplexed with sorrow in their hearts, who awake each morning in fear and apprehension of what the day brings—if you can help one soul to find some serenity and to realize that he/she is not neglected, but surrounded by arms of infinite love, that is a great work. It is more important than anything else.

Silver Birch

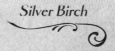

SPIRIT SPEAKS

About the Author

Michael Mayo has been studying mediumship for more than fifteen years. He created his own online school, the Oakbridge Institute, where he teaches progressive foundational mediumship courses to students all over the world. He has also taught through the Shift Network.

A Step-by-Step & Evidence-Based Approach
to Genuine Spirit Communication

SPIRIT
SPEAKS

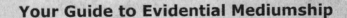

Your Guide to Evidential Mediumship

MICHAEL MAYO

Llewellyn Publications
Woodbury, Minnesota

FIRST EDITION
First Printing, 2022

Book design by Rebecca Zins
Cover design by Kevin R. Brown

Llewellyn is a registered trademark of Llewellyn Worldwide Ltd.

Library of Congress Cataloging-In-Publication Data
Pending
ISBN 978-0-7387-7343-8

Llewellyn Publications
A Division of Llewellyn Worldwide Ltd.
2143 Wooddale Drive
Woodbury, MN 55125-2989

www.llewellyn.com
Printed in the United States of America

Dedicated to

Barbara B. Myles, my first teacher, who
gave me patience, friendship, and love.

Gordon Smith, who took me from
believing in spirit to knowing its reality.

Eileen Davies, who unlocked my mediumship and
shared her wisdom, time, and encouragement.

James Van Praagh, who paved the way, guided,
and showed me how to be a success.

Contents

Letter to the Developing Medium   xix

Introduction   1

How This Book Is Set Up and How It Can Help You   3

My Journey   4

Why I Wrote This Book   11

Part 1

Clarifying Genuine Mediumship

1: Dispelling Common Myths and Fears   15

What a Medium Is…and Isn't   16

Cultural-Based Myths   16

Religious-Based Myths   21

Media-Based Myths   24

An Alternate Perspective on Negative Spiritual Experiences   31

Evil and Negative Spirits   31

Possession and Exorcism   36

Spiritual or Psychological?   37

Curses and Attachments   40

Myths About the Afterlife   44

Being Stuck or Lost   46

Rescue Circles   47

Suicide   48

Contents

2: Understanding the Authentic Medium's Experience   51

What to Expect on Your Mediumship Journey   51

Working with the Power   55

The Clairs   57

Clairvoyance   57

Clairaudience   58

Clairsentience   58

Claircognizance   59

Psychism vs. Mediumship   59

Remaining Grounded for Genuine Spiritual Connection   62

Misleading Behaviors   62

Addressing Toxic Positivity   63

Empaths   64

Avoiding Cold Reading, Hot Reading, and Mentalism   67

Cold Reading   67

Hot Reading   68

Mentalism   68

Part 2

Historical Mediums and Forms of Mediumship

3: The Many Ways in Which Mediumship Can Show Itself   73

Mental Mediumship   74

Physical Mediumship   74

Trance Mediumship   76

Trance Philosophy   77

Trance Clairvoyance   77

Trance Communication   77

Trance Art   77

Automatic Writing   78

Healing Mediumship   78

Energy Healing   78

Trance Healing   79

4: Exceptional Mediums of the Past   81

Examples of Mental Mediums   81

Helen Hughes   82

Albert Best   83

Examples of Physical Mediums   83

Jack Webber   83

Alec Harris   84

Leslie Flint   84

Examples of Trance Mediums   85

Maurice Barbanell   85

Gladys Osborne Leonard   85

Helen Hughes   86

José Medrado   87

Leonora Piper   88

Examples of Healing Mediums   88

George Chapman   88

Harry Edwards   89

Part 3

Before You Begin

5: Ethics of Mediumship and Psychic Work   93

Boundaries   95

Understand Your Limits   97

Fear-Based Readings   97

Unethical Information: Predicting Death,
    Disease, Divorce, or Disaster   98

Ethics of Development   99

**6: Understand Potential Sources of Tension
So You Can Surrender   101**

Desire   102

Distraction   104

Expectation   108

Contents

7: Become Familiar with Grief   111

    Remain Compassionate and Nonjudgmental   113

    The Five Stages of Grief   114

        Denial   115

        Anger   115

        Bargaining   115

        Depression   115

        Acceptance   116

    Allow Grief to Be Processed   116

    Mediums Experience Grief, Too   118

    Grief Can Make It Difficult to Connect   118

Part 4

A Step-by-Step Approach to Developing Mediumship

8: Begin by Working with the Power   123

    How Working with the Power Feels   123

    Why It's Important   124

    The Power of the Spirit vs. Your Personal Power   125

    Sitting In the Power   127

    How It Differs from Meditation   130

    EXERCISE: **Sitting In the Power**   131

9: Making Sense of the Sensations You Experience   137

    Attunement   137

    EXERCISE: **Attunement Process**   138

    Narration   139

    EXERCISE: **Practicing Narration**   140

        Take Time for Reflection   141

10: Connecting with Your Spirit Guides   143

    What Is a Spirit Guide?   144

    My Experience of Meeting My Guide   145

What Guides Do vs. What They Don't Do   149

EXERCISE: Learning to Sense and Feel Your Guide   151

11: Connecting with Spirit Communicators   155

Structure of a Reading   155

Opening Prayer   156

Attunement   157

Opening Spiel   157

Moving Into the Power   160

Making a Link   161

The Triangle of Communication   161

Reading Tips   164

Take It Moment to Moment   164

Put Aside Desire, Distraction, and Expectation   164

Intend It, Don't Will It   164

Describe, Don't Interpret   165

Follow the Yeses   166

EXERCISE: Experience Connecting with
a Spirit Communicator   167

12: Learning to Recognize Spirit People by Their Essence   169

EXERCISE: Sensing Physical Essence   170

People Are Complex   171

EXERCISE: Discovering Where and How
You Feel the Essence   173

Checking In with Your Feeling Space   175

13: Discerning and Delivering Quality Evidence   177

Types of Evidential Information   178

List Information   178

Personal Evidence   180

What Quality Evidence Is Not   181

Information That Can't Be Validated   181

Psychic Information   182

Fear-Based, Predictive, or Interfering Information   183

Information That's Lacking Context   184

Contents

How to Get Quality Evidence   185

    Feeling Essence First   185

    Describing the Changes as They Happen   186

    Exploring Layers of the Communication   188

EXERCISE: **Making a Clear and Evidential Link with a Spirit Communicator   193**

14: Sharing the Message from Loved Ones in Spirit   197

What Constitutes a Message   198

What Is Not a Message   198

Things That Might Be Included   200

Examples of Quality Messages   201

EXERCISE: **Message-Focused Reading   204**

    Take Time for Reflection   205

15: Troubleshooting Readings   207

Issues Stemming from the Medium   207

    How to Handle "No"   208

    Losing the Link   210

    Switching—Is This More Than One Spirit?   212

    When You Get Nothing   215

Sensitive Issues   217

Issues Stemming from the Sitter   219

    Difficult Sitters   220

    Skeptical Sitters   220

    Sitters Who Want Something Specific   222

Issues Stemming from the Spirit Communicator   224

Conclusion   227

Recommended Resources   231

Letter to the Developing Medium

As you begin to embark on this exciting journey into yourself and the spirit world, I offer you some words of guidance gleaned from many years of my own development as well as the many years of watching my students unfold their spiritual abilities.

Mediumship is a serious endeavor with a lot of responsibility. We are often working with people in varying states of bereavement and loss; what we say, how we say it, and when we say it matters. Be impeccable with your words and hold yourself to a high degree of moral and ethical standards. Integrity is everything in this work—in respect to others, ourselves, and our obligation to the spirit world. Live your life in integrity to the best of your ability.

Mediumship development takes time. As I always tell my students, "Rome wasn't built in a day and neither is your mediumship." It is through time, patience, and dedication that we are blessed with the gifts of the spirit. Trust in the process, and do not be attached to an end goal or arrival point. Doing so will ultimately lead to frustration and self-judgment. As cliché as it sounds, the journey really is the goal. It is where all learning comes from.

Understand the "why" of your development and revisit it regularly. Too often people's egos transform well-intentioned mediums into ego-driven showmen. Keep the humble heart of service as paramount and remember that this is a sacred calling; never lose sight of your compassion for others, for all will know grief in this life if you are here long enough.

A properly developed medium is not "on" all the time. Turning your perception of the spirit world off is just as important, if not more important, as turning it on. Do not be confused by the media's portrayal of the "spirit-plagued medium" who is obliged to pass on every message before they're "freed of the spirit's torment." As my mentor Gordon Smith always says, "No one is a victim of spirit." You are *always* in control of your mediumship and your perception.

Live in the real world. Be careful not to treat your spirituality as an excuse to escape the challenges of daily life. We come to this earth to learn lessons. If everything was meant to be rosy and peaceful, we would have stayed in the world of spirit. Spiritualize yourself but remember part of that development comes from overcoming life's challenges, too. Let your mediumship bolster your own personal perseverance, not replace it. Take responsibility for your life.

Your mental health matters as much as your spiritual awareness. Your needs matter. Those drawn to mediumship are often givers and sensitives. You cannot be of any use to others if you are exhausted physically, mentally, and emotionally. Put on your oxygen mask before helping others put on theirs! Your spiritual path and your personal healing path are two separate roads; tend to them both.

Use reasoned, sound judgment in all you do, especially your spiritual journey. Be practical and even-tempered. Do not believe something just because someone says so (even me!). Try it on. If it helps you, keep it; if it doesn't, throw it away. If it causes you fear or self-doubt, it is not of the spirit. Fear has no place in mediumship. The spirit is love.

Spirit is here to support, not dictate. Spirit does not wish to run your life or tell you how something should be done. That is your job. Do not turn to spirit for every trivial thing as it damages discernment between the mind and what is coming from the spirit world. Trust that if it is important, the spirit will let you know. That being said, spirit cannot give us all the answers to everything. Have the humility to accept that some things are beyond our awareness. We are not meant to know everything.

It is okay to be wrong. The fear of failure or of being a "fraud" is the greatest stumbling block for new mediums. The sooner you learn to accept that you are a fallible human and that that is okay, the sooner you will be set free. Perseverance and patience are the cornerstones to anything worth doing. Mediumship is no different. You won't always get it right, but each no or wrong answer will teach you something and bring you closer to another yes.

Lastly, learn to trust yourself. One of the most common phrases I hear from students is "I trust spirit; I just don't trust myself." The sooner you learn to trust yourself in all things, success and "failure," the sooner your mediumship will flourish. As my teacher Mrs. Davies always says, "Your trust is the gift you give the other world." Give it to yourself as well!

Introduction

Why be a medium?

That's the question I posed to a mediumship development circle of mine. What draws you to mediumship? Why take time and energy out of your life to learn this skill? What do you want to do with it?

We went around the circle one by one, introducing ourselves to the group and sharing the answer to these rather personal questions. The first person shared their story of being drawn to it at a very young age and how they've always had an interest in the subject. The next one discussed the desire to help people. Another expressed that they always felt like an outcast for not fitting into the "regular world" and not being understood, to which several of the participants nodded their heads in agreement. Others discussed having unexplainable experiences when they were younger, which inspired them to search for answers. "That's a hard one," puzzled another. "I think my reasons have changed over time. I think right now it just makes me feel good." Around the circle we went, each of the fifteen or so participants sharing their stories and experiences, some even welling up with emotions as they spoke.

What amazed me about this group was that they all spoke so openly, honestly, and from the heart. This mattered to them—it carried weight, and we couldn't help but feel the power in these stories. Emotions of understanding, harmony, and support for one another permeated the space, and by the end of the introductions, everyone was feeling uplifted, connected, and harmonious—the perfect conditions for connecting with spirit, of course! But more than that, I had an opportunity to hear the common themes among those who are drawn or called to the path of mediumship. To many, mediumship offered a clear and evidential way of connecting with something greater than themselves. Some call that God, Source, or Universe; I call it the Great Spirit. By whatever name it is given, there seemed to be an innate desire to personally know this source that is greater than the self. The participants described how mediumship allowed them to have faith in their connection to spirit as well as have real, tangible experiences of its reality.

Along with this theme, mediumship provided people with the evidence that life continues on beyond the doorway we call death. I find that the loss of a loved one is the most common reason that people begin to give mediumship a serious look. In their grief, they search for answers and begin to question, "Where do we go after this? Does this consciousness live on beyond death—not in some airy-fairy cloudy heaven but in a more immediate and present-time reality?" For many of the participants, mediumship offered answers as well as the evidence to support them.

Community was another commonly cited reason for having an interest in mediumship—particularly our ongoing circle. One of the core tenets of any mediumship development circle is the rule that harmony among participants is paramount. Through this harmony and love, the correct conditions are created for spirit to easily come forward and connect with us. The byproduct of this is that those who are in circle together each week are building a sense of connection, camaraderie, and friendship with one another. For many that felt outcast or like they didn't fit in the regular world, these kinds of groups make them feel understood, recognized, and part of something meaningful.

The desire to help and uplift others was the most cited reason for wanting to develop mediumship. "It would just feel so fulfilling to be able to help people out of their grief and bring comfort" was a sentiment that was shared several times, and I think that this is the most meaningful of the bunch. Mediumship at its core is about healing. There is no greater feeling in this work than when you see the light of recognition spark in the eyes of your client. The death of a loved one often feels so final, like the phone has been hung up on someone forever. Where did they go? Are they okay? Are they still aware of me now? So many questions often feel left unanswered. The gift of the medium is to be able to offer answers to these questions—to help the recipient remember the life of their loved one in spirit and allow themselves to move beyond the death, which is where so many often remain stuck. It is recognizing that our journeys do not end when we shed our physical form, and that in some ways our loved ones in spirit are closer now than they ever have been before. Perhaps most important is the knowledge that we will see our loved ones in spirit again.

Whether you picked up this book to discover more about yourself, connect with a loved one of your own, or develop your own skills as a medium, my hope is that you will approach it with an open mind, an open heart, and a willingness to step outside of your comfort zone of what you think you already know. I hope that you can set aside your expectations and desires, come to the Great Spirit with an empty cup that is waiting to be filled, and leave your ego at the door. Mediumship is a lifelong journey of unfolding, and this book is meant to be a stepping-stone in that journey. Be patient with yourself and your process of unfoldment. As my mentor Eileen Davies always says, "When the inner and outer conditions are right, the flower will bloom."

How This Book Is Set Up and How It Can Help You

This book is set up to be used as a progressive learning course, taking you from the beginnings of your mediumistic journey to making a link with the spirit world and beyond. I will be taking you through a step-by-step approach to connecting with spirit that I have used for many years in my development circles with great success. Even if you already have experience with your mediumship, the exercises and philosophy shared in this book can often fill any gaps you may have and take your mediumship to the next level. This book will provide you with a solid understanding of the mechanics of mediumship (the how-tos of spirit communication) while also providing a history of mediumship, ethical considerations, and an understanding of grief and grieving.

Several chapters will offer exercises for you to do that can be done alone or with a group of people. While this book can be used as a self-taught course on your own, learning mediumship in a group is always preferable to learning by yourself. If you don't have anyone else to work through this book with, you can find support in online circles or in local development circles (more on how to select a good circle and teacher later). Some folks may not have access to these circles, which is why I have created an online school for mediumship called the Oakbridge Institute.[1] Here you will find classes, workshops, and a like-minded community to help you on your journey.

Whether alone or with others, this book will be your guide to clear, accurate, and genuine spirit communication.

My Journey

The journey of discovering one's mediumistic potential is unique and varied. For some, it begins early in childhood. Read almost any biography on most mediums and you will be met with fabulous stories of early childhood experiences that tipped them off on their mediumistic potential (see recommended resources). Floating heads in closets, spirit people vying for their attention, some not-so-imaginary friends, miraculous apparitions that vanish as quickly as they appear, visions of lights around people's heads, and much more often fill these pages. And while these stories are fantastic and awe inspiring, they are not my lived experience at all...not even a little bit. As exciting as floating heads and ghostly apparitions would be, my youth was comparatively unremark-

---

1   https://www.oakbridgeinstitute.org/

able. What I did carry with me, however, was an early desire and awareness to know this thing people called God. One of my earliest memories is asking a family friend if they would teach me about God—a pretty strange thing for a child from a nonreligious household to be asking about, but the passion for it has never waned.

It is this desire to know the divine that led me to search for the truth about who and what we are. Along the way, I have had the pleasure of coming across many different answers and perspectives to these questions. While exploring various belief systems and doctrines, I had always looked for something very specific: evidence. Proof, in some real or tangible way, that what those claiming to know the truth about the nature of God and reality was accurate. While I feel that I gained valuable experiences through each viewpoint I tried on, I was always left with more questions than answers, and where the answers fell short, I was often told to just "have faith" or that I "just didn't believe enough." Surely, if there was a divine intelligence beyond all of this, they would not need to be so elusive, cryptic, or unclear, and so my search continued for many years.

Not knowing what to do with myself after high school, I decided to attend massage therapy school. Little did I know that this choice would set off a series of events that would start me on a path to the answers I had been searching for all this time. As is often the case, you never know which choice you make will be the one that changes your life forever. After class one afternoon, one of the instructors was using oracle cards and crystals to do a psychic reading for another student. Fascinated, I decided to find a place that sold crystals somewhere in my area. I ended up at a small metaphysical bookstore called, appropriately enough, Awakenings Bookstore.

When I entered, I was greeted by the friendly shop owner, who happily explained cards, crystals, and more to me. Excited and intrigued to explore further, I returned the next day. When I arrived, the owner was there again. As we got to talking, he suggested that I attend an event happening that evening called a "demonstration of mediumship." I had never heard of this before, so I asked him what it was. He explained that in a demonstration, a medium stands at the front of a room and gives messages to people in the audience from their departed loved ones. I was fascinated by this, though I didn't think that the medium would call on me as at that point in my life, I had not had anyone close to me pass away. Regardless of this fact, I decided to attend.

When I arrived later that night, there were roughly fifty people in the room. I took a seat at the very front and waited uncomfortably for the demonstration to begin. I felt a bit out of place, but I wanted to see what this was all about. Once everyone was settled in their seats, the same friendly shop owner came in and introduced the medium for the evening. He was from the UK and used to be a detective until he began to have spiritual experiences of crossed-over loved ones that he could no longer ignore. He was a very unassuming gentleman, and with his gentle way and soft voice, he began to give messages to people in the audience. He called on a lady and began to deliver information that she could understand. He provided many details about the person in spirit that were all validated by the woman. I found it interesting but I was also a bit skeptical. How could I truly know if the things he was saying were true? As the evening went on, he continued to call on people in the audience and deliver messages of survival and love, all of which were reportedly accurate and correct.

About a third of the way through the meeting, I was startled into attention when he began speaking to me! He asked if I was aware of an older gentleman in spirit, which he believed to be my grandfather. I told him that my grandfather was living. He then suggested that perhaps it was my great-grandfather, but I quickly told him I never knew him. Slightly puzzled, he joked, "Well, he's clearly here for some reason." He checked back in with the spirit communicator and stated, "Are you aware you are very psychic?" to which I nervously replied yes, only because I had had dreams that had come true. I did not really know to what extent he meant.

He continued the message. "This man is wanting me to tell you that you are very psychic and that you need to start developing your mediumship, and that one day, you will be up here doing what I am doing right now." At that moment it felt like time stopped. He continued on with information about how to access these gifts, but at that point I wasn't listening anymore. I was both shocked and confused as I had never had an inclination for any kind of mediumistic awareness before! In a daze, I thanked him for the message and got lost in thought. I have no memory of the rest of the demonstration or any awareness of what other messages were given that night. Afterward, as I came out of my haze, many people came up to me asking me if I offered readings or if I was interested in studying with them. Overwhelmed, I left the room and returned to the main part of the bookstore. I saw the friendly shop owner again, and he commented on the message I had received. He suggested that I go to the psychic development circle that was on Monday nights to begin developing the gift I had no idea I had.

Having had my interest piqued, I attended the psychic development circle a few weeks later. It was run by a lady who would eventually become my first teacher for many years, Barbara. She was an attractive, warm, and fun woman who made her development circle feel safe and harmonious. A development circle is where mediums learn to connect with the spirit world and hone their spiritual abilities. There were roughly eight or so people in the circle that evening. We began with discussion, and Barbara was filled with great information about something called clairs, chakras, and energy. While I didn't fully understand how it all worked, I found myself soaking it all up. Then she led us through a guided meditation. I remember feeling at peace and centered after that experience—the class was worth attending for the meditation alone! We finally came to the exercise portion of the evening, and Barbara had us reading another student as they stood against a blank wall. The intention of the exercise was to sense and see the aura, but any kind of information was welcomed.

When it was my turn, I stood there staring at the lady standing against the wall. Barbara prompted me to just relax and speak whatever was coming to my mind. Not having ever done this before, I had no expectation as to what or how it was supposed to feel or be. I followed her prompt exactly and just allowed myself to become relaxed and passive. As I did this, I began to feel a sense of my awareness changing, almost like the feeling of zoning out. Then I began to feel like a man was standing next to me. Since that was all I was experiencing, I began with, "There's a man here"—and just as I began to say that, more information began to come in—"and he says his name is Jorge."

Surprised, the lady said, "Yes! I can take that."

More information continued to come. "He says that you were friends and that he passed in the month of March."

Even more surprised, the lady smiled and exclaimed, "Yes! Wow. That's right."

I continued to pass information without any real idea how I was getting it other than knowing it was the next thing coming to my mind. "He says that you were very close and his passing was sudden—an accident."

"Yes—wow, he's good!" she shot back. I continued to pass on more and more information, all of which she could take. In hindsight it could be considered an ideal reading in its clarity and specificity. When I finished, I remember returning to normal awareness, with Barbara looking at me quite pleased and other students surprised and happy for me. Here was this eighteen-year-old kid attending his first class and delivering an accurate mediumship message. I remember thinking as I returned to my seat, "Huh…I guess that medium guy was right."

The next week I returned to the circle feeling confident, excited, and ready to see what else I could get. It seemed like I really was a medium after all and it came so easily and naturally last time; surely this time will be just as easy. Once we got to the exercise portion of the class, I confidently and happily stood up to give what I was getting. However, this time, when I waited for information to start coming, nothing came. Slightly embarrassed, I did not deliver any messages that night. "Maybe it will work better next week," I wondered. The next week came, and yet again I got nothing. The following week came; again, nothing! What was happening? Why did it not work when I wanted it to? What was so different about the first time from all these other times?

Having seen that it worked before, and with the encouragement from Barbara to continue, I decided to pursue my development and learn how to get it to work again. This began several years of dedicated weekly attendance to this circle. In time the information began to return, though during this development period it was never as clear as the first message I had given. Looking back now, I can recognize what occurred (which I will explain in detail in later chapters) and how the stumbling block was my mind and my expectation. But this experience was enough to ignite the lifelong journey to discover what my potential was as a psychic medium. I knew I could do it; I just needed to learn how to do it on command. It was almost as if the spirit had dangled a carrot in front of me and said, "This is what's possible. Now go develop it."

While it was frustrating at times, the beauty of the journey far outweighed the struggle. I was finally given real, tangible evidence that there was a spiritual reality I could interact with. Given the right conditions both mentally and physically, I could consistently access a connection to a greater divine essence that truly was eternal and that I could learn from. I had finally found what I was looking for all those years.

Since that first message prophesied so many years ago—"One day you'll be up here doing what I'm doing"—I have been blessed with its fulfillment. I have had the great pleasure of providing thousands of healing messages to people all over the world. Through private sittings, small groups, and large demonstrations, the medium's words came true. In fact, I stood in that very room and gave a demonstration of mediumship.

The spirit world has always supported me on my journey in my development and has led me to some of the greatest mediums and teachers working today. Through their tutelage, my mediumship has flourished and has inspired me to teach others what I have learned along the way. After many years of teaching students in development circles, private mentoring, and workshops, I have had the pleasure to create my own mediumship development school online, the Oakbridge Institute. We are currently working on a retreat-style physical location to create a safe and supportive environment to develop your spiritual connection. Who knows? We just might get to work together there soon!

I always like to share my story of how I discovered my mediumistic ability because it illustrates key points that I believe are important takeaways. Contrary to other mediums, I never knew that I had any mediumistic ability until someone told me I could do it. That belief in myself was enough to open something up that allowed me to have an amazing experience. Therefore, we see that belief in your ability is paramount to your success in mediumship development: accept that you can do this. Which brings me to the second takeaway: there was nothing in my early life that indicated I was a medium, which means just because you might not have had dramatic spiritual experiences in your youth, that does not indicate you are any less mediumistic. Mediumship is not something that is reserved for the special; rather, it is a natural byproduct of being a soul having a human experience. Anyone can develop some level of mediumistic awareness. It is your birthright as a spiritual being.

Lastly, the journey of unfolding will have its highs and lows—sometimes it will not work the way it did before—but that does not make you any less of a medium. As I often tell my students, a kicker on a football team kicks field goals. Sometimes he misses; does that make him any less of a kicker? No, he still does his best and continues to develop his skill. It is through dedication and time that we get past these blocks and reveal what is truly possible for us. Do not get discouraged by a few readings that go awry. Each one is there to teach you something. Let yourself be open to falling and getting back up—that's the journey of the medium. And in case no one has told you this before, allow me to be the first to say you can do this, and you *are* a medium!

Why I Wrote This Book

Of all the work that I do with the spirit world, teaching is my greatest passion. Through my years of searching and journeying through all the information that is out there on the topic of mediumship and psychic development, I truly believe that I have distilled and filtered out the unnecessary portions, and I am left with what brings about clear, accurate, and specific information in the most efficient manner. This is my reasoning for writing this book. I wanted to take my sixteen-plus years of mediumistic and psychical experiences and offer what I have learned in a succinct, clear, and step-by-step approach that will lead my fellow truth seekers to the answers I spent so long looking for.

Working in the field of spiritual development as long as I have, I've come to realize it is a bit of a free-for-all. There seems to be a sense that anything goes within the realms of the "spiritual." And while I can hold space for that perspective, when it comes to getting clear and accurate information in mediumship and psychic readings, I have found that there are concrete concepts and ideas that, when applied, consistently produce repeatable, positive results. Moreover, there are specific, commonly taught techniques put forward by instructors and within circles of information, both online and in instructional institutions, that I have found actively *discourage* the development of mediumship. For example, instructors often pressure students to actively search to "get more" detail on a piece of information that they are given. This kind of technique encourages the mind and does not allow the medium to follow the lead of the spirit. Sure, this may work for some, but what I am interested in are the underlying universal core concepts of what make mediumship and psychism work. What are the mechanisms that create the miracle of communication, and how do we learn to enter into this receptive state of awareness on command? If we can understand the underlying modulators of psychic and mediumistic awareness, we can, in theory, consistently produce clear connections with the spirit world. This book allows me to lay out my system and theory on how and why mediumship works so that you can apply it in your own work with the spirit.

Even more importantly than efficient and effective techniques to get accurate information from the spirit world, I want to dispel the misinformation out there that at best creates unnecessary fear and at worst can potentially harm or hurt people. Is my loved one stuck because of suicide? Did they cross over to the spirit world? Are they suffering where they are? These are all questions that derive from information that has been passed through the media and fear-based philosophy of the world of spirit. By clearing up these untruths, we gain access to a much more accurate picture of the spirit world; as a byproduct, we experience the gifts that the spirit world brings us when we connect with it: peace, harmony, support, and love.

Through a deeper understanding of how we can accurately receive clear and specific information, dispelling unnecessary beliefs, and recognizing what genuine spiritual connection provides, we are able to begin exploring our true spiritual nature. Deepening this understanding allows us to spiritualize ourselves—that is, connect with who we truly are beyond the stories and roles we play within this lifetime. We are met by the part of us that is eternal, and as a byproduct of this awareness, we begin to live our lives in a much more meaningful and conscious way. We also begin to recognize that becoming a medium is about much more than passing on messages from those on the higher side of life. It is an important stepping-stone in our journey into who we truly are and in what way we have come to leave a mark here on this earth. I hope to pass on to you my personal observations and pearls of wisdom I have acquired along the way that may help you in deepening your understanding of yourself and who you truly are as a spiritual being.

Part 1

Clarifying Genuine Mediumship

1

Dispelling Common Myths and Fears

If you were to walk into the street and begin to survey any passersby about what they believe a medium is, you are likely to get as many differing answers as you do people that you speak to. This is because mediums are often defined based on what people are exposed to from the environment around them. Whether that is from the media, religous, or cultural experiences, our view of mediumship varies from villain to saint.

Even within mediumship communities, there is confusion or disagreement over what constitutes a medium and what they actually do. Combine this with social media "experts" on networks such as TikTok and Instagram, and the level of misinformation and opinion is astounding. As we begin to explore this topic, it is therefore vital for us to clear up any confusion, misconceptions, and outright incorrect information about working with the spirit world.

As I often tell my students, mediumship is hard enough to develop without extraneous and unnecessary beliefs and practices that will only complicate connecting with the spirit. Mediumship should be simple. Anything that adds to the process will only inhibit growth and slow down development. Trust me: having to learn how to manage your thinking mind when working mediumistically is already plenty of work that takes years to fully get ahold of—and even then it is a constant practice to keep it at bay!

To this end, I believe it is important for me to clarify, to the best of my ability, some of the most common misconceptions and ideas surrounding mediumship, readings, and the spirit world. The concepts and perspectives I intend to offer you are gathered from years of theoretical and practical applications in thousands of hours of readings, demonstrations, healings, and experimentation within my own mediumship and connection to the spirit world. I also have been very blessed to have been led to some of the most accurate and incredible mediums we have living today. Through their combined seventy-plus years of experience working with the world of spirit, as well as my own lived experience, I can confidently say that the perspectives I will share with you are accurate and will support you in your understanding of your own mediumship.

What a Medium Is ... and Isn't

Clearing up misconceptions about what a medium is or is not is an important place to start. By exploring the three most common areas where we receive ideas about mediums—our culture, religion, and media—we can begin to separate fact from fiction and help deepen our understanding of what mediumship and mediums are like. Below are some of the most common misconceptions I hear about mediums.

Cultural-Based Myths

As I mentioned before, the ideas we have about mediums are largely due to our environmental influences. Culture plays a huge role in our beliefs around how we view mediums. Western culture, in particular, has both romanticized and demonized mediums, often portraying them as either magical beings with the ability to live in two worlds at once or outright frauds out to make a buck.

The reality is that most mediums are compassionate people who wish to do good and help those who have been touched by grief. Oftentimes their own journeys have begun because of a great personal loss. It is important for us to recognize that mediums are also humans and are fallible. We are no more special than your average person. The only difference is that we poured our time, energy, and resources into cultivating a skill to learn to sense the subtle energy around us and be of service to others.

Mediums are fortunetellers—While mediums can sometimes be made aware of things that come through with the help of loved ones in spirit, mediums are not fortunetellers. Plenty of cultural and media portrayals of mediums depict them as older women wearing turbans, crystals, and scarves, staring at a crystal ball in a dimly lit room, asking you to cross their palm with silver for a reading on your love life. And while turbans and crystals are a fun option, mediums are not here to tell you what your boyfriend is thinking about you, what career you should pick, or what the winning lotto numbers will be.

Mediums specifically communicate with loved ones in spirit. They develop their skill to tune into the energy of a spirit communicator and then describe their experience of them. They should be able to bring forward information that you would understand about your loved one's life, i.e., personality, names, dates, shared memories, important events, places, passing conditions, etc. When you feel satisfied that your loved one is present, they can then pass you any messages that your loved one may have for you.

Mediums know everything/have all the answers—As lovely as that might sound, mediums cannot give you all the answers to your life's problems. Not only is that not possible, it also would do your soul no good if for every struggle you came across, a medium gave you the solution to it. Your life is for you to live, not to be dictated by anyone else. You came here to go through the highs and lows of life so that your soul could develop and learn. That will be incredibly uncomfortable at times. It is your journey and your lessons to master and overcome. It is through challenge that we evolve and grow beyond what we think we are capable of.

What a medium can do is tell you what your loved ones in spirit have to share with you. This can be very healing or even, at times, provide some guidance on choices you may make in your life—no different than when you call up a loved one for advice. The choices are ultimately yours to make as the spirit world is not interested in dictating how your life should go. Your loved ones in spirit are there to support you and help you in any way that they can, but they won't be upset if you make the choice you want to make. Like all advice in life, if it is helpful, sound, and true, consider it. If it is not, throw it out!

Mediums are mind readers—While mediums can often sense the energy around someone and become aware of information about them, we cannot read your mind. Mind reading would fall under telepathy, which is an extrasensory perceptive faculty that we would classify under psychism. And while mediums are also often quite psychic, it is not what we spend our years of development doing. Instead, we develop our ability to sense the subtle energy of spirit communicators and then describe our experience.

Moreover, mediums regularly bring through information that would rule out mind reading as a possible explanation for what we are doing. We call this kind of information "research evidence." In research evidence, the medium provides information that is not known by the sitter (the person receiving the reading). The sitter then must go and ask someone else who might know. Oftentimes during a reading the medium will receive a reply from a sitter that a piece of information given was incorrect, only to receive a message after the reading that the sitter checked in with another loved one and they confirmed that piece of information. Research evidence is an excellent indication of the continuation of consciousness of your loved one in spirit.

Mediums are always "on"—It is commonly thought that a medium is always sensitive and connected to the spirit world. This is not the case. A well-developed medium will only turn on their mediumistic ability when they are working in a reading or demonstration. Mediums spend the early part of their development learning how to turn it on and off, which is vital for proper discernment between what is coming from their mind versus what is coming from the spirit.

You will often hear some "mediums" say that they are constantly getting information from the spirit world. This is an indication of a medium who has not developed boundaries or proper control of their desire to connect with the spirit world. It is the desire of the medium to connect with the spirit world that keeps the channel open. These "leaky faucet" mediums are prone to passing information to basically anyone who will listen at any time. When the underdeveloped medium learns that it is their "checking in" to see if spirit is present, they will begin to gain control over their ability and be able to turn it off at will. Other reasons that they may be staying open are commonly due to their ego wanting to feel special or validated. Also, some developing mediums were never taught that they should turn it off. Turning it off is just as important, if not more, as turning it on.

All mediums are frauds—This answer requires a qualifier: most genuine mediums are not frauds. I say "most" because a genuine medium can go from being a genuine medium with real ability to a genuine medium with real ability who also cheats just by researching information prior to a reading. I give this strange answer largely because mediumship has historically and in present day been wrought with frauds (more on this in later chapters).

That being said, genuine mediums with integrity do exist and are more common than not! Quality developed mediums spend years of their lives in meditation and development circles honing their ability to access information not readily available to our physical senses. It is through this rigorous training that they are able to bring forward astoundingly clear, specific, and accurate information—oftentimes information that is unresearchable. I have had the greatest pleasure of witnessing—both in my own work and in the work of my mentors and colleagues—information in languages unbeknownst to the medium: names of places they had never been to or heard of, full street addresses, shared memories, nicknames used between loved ones, code words agreed upon prior to the passing of a loved one that they promised they would mention if they were able to communicate from the other side, and much more. The key is patient, consistent development over time. This is the hallmark of high-quality mediumship.

Mediums see and hear spirit as clear as living people—For some mediums, hearing the spirit world as crystal clear as Whoopi Goldberg did in the movie *Ghost* is a real thing! So is the way Haley Joel Osment saw Bruce Willis in *The Sixth Sense*. However, this experience of mediumship is very rare (objective clairaudience and objective clairvoyance, respectively). For most of us, we experience the spirit communicator through multiple senses: feeling, seeing, knowing, and hearing. These impressions come to us as fleeting, quick experiences that we have to communicate and describe to the best of our ability so that our sitter, the person receiving the reading, understands the information. While many of us do have the ability to hear the spirit, it is often words or sometimes sentences rather than full streams of consciousness passing through word for word. This is why we spend many years in development: to grow our ability so that we might strengthen these senses and thereby develop clearer and more specific impressions from the spirit communicator.

Religious-Based Myths

One of the more challenging areas to tackle are the viewpoints brought about by religious beliefs. Oftentimes those who come from a religious background carry a lot of fear and anxiety about connecting with the world of spirit, even if they are no longer affiliated with their original religious beliefs. It is important for anyone seriously interested in developing their mediumship to evaluate their past beliefs about spirit communication. While many religious texts do condemn the practice, they seem to only do so when it is not done in the name of a specific deity.

For example, in 1 Corinthians 12:4–10, Paul the Apostle writes to the Corinthians of the many gifts available to those who follow Christ. For those who are moved by the Holy Spirit, some are gifted healing, others prophecy, others discerning spirits, while others speak in tongues. These are all the same exact gifts that we, as mediums, experience when moving into what we call "the power." The experience is interchangeable, but the difference is that one is interpreted through the lens of a specific system of belief; the other is not. My belief is that they are all experiencing the same mystical experience that derives from removing one's own mind and desires in an act of service to a greater good and a higher power. If we can take something from this example about our true nature, it is that we are more than just a body; we are also a spirit that is connected to something greater than ourselves, regardless of what we believe.

With this in mind, I would encourage those who still carry these fears to recognize that it is human beings who put labels on things to try to make sense of them. The beauty of connecting with the divine is still the same, regardless of the lens and scope through which we choose to view it. Free yourself from dogma and fear-based beliefs as you step into genuine connection with the divine force that is in all things.

Mediums are in partnership with the devil—On this point I can speak from personal experience. In no instance in my sixteen-year journey have I ever experienced anything negative, scary, or bad coming from the world of spirit. Through working with the spirit, we come to recognize that communication with the other world is strengthened by feelings of love, harmony, compassion, and fraternity. These feelings create a vibration that heals and helps those who participate in this connection. It is because of this that I know mediums do not consort with any kind of negative being (if they exist in the first place). In fact, if anything, the source of our mediumistic awareness is something that is innate with our own spiritual beingness—the divinity and connection to the Great Spirit that resides within us. You already have within you a mediumistic potential; all you have to do is tap into it.

It is easy to point to something one does not understand and deem it evil. It requires no inspection, critical thinking, or questioning of oneself or beliefs. To blindly follow is easy. To question and discover for yourself is harder.

Mediums are communicating with demons—Similar to the last myth, mediums do not work with demons. Some people argue that demons are pretending to be your loved one in spirit to lead the believers astray. First, let us stop for a moment to consider this. In my many years of working with mediumship, the results of my work have always been profound healing, growth, peace, forgiveness, and closure. The job of the medium is to provide an opportunity for healing for those who are lost in grief so that they might engage in life again. The very notion that this is somehow the result of demonic intervention seems laughable—that is, unless the goal of these demons is to create healing, relief, peace, and a return of joy back into people's lives, which seems contrary to the whole idea of demons. Moreover, I find this idea completely heartless and cruel to tell someone who is grieving— that not only have they lost someone they love, but now dark forces are at work to trick them. It is just not right. If anyone ever tries to tell you this, please recognize their ignorance and be on your way.

Going to a medium disturbs your loved one in the afterlife—I have sometimes heard the concern that we are disturbing the peace of those who have crossed to the other side. I can understand why some people may carry this worry. When someone passes, we often have practices and rituals that we do to allow our loved one to find a sense of peace and rest, as in the term "laid to rest" or "rest in peace." However, I can assure you that it was the spirits of those who love us who started the communication! Those in spirit are often eager to let us know that they are still around and aware of us and that they are okay! Our loved ones on the higher side of life are aware that we are grieving their loss, and they want to make contact with us to bring us comfort and let us know, "Hey! I'm okay!" Wouldn't you? In my experience, those in spirit are excited to reconnect with those they love to bring reassurance and comfort to those left behind. As my mentor Gordon Smith always says, "Death is for the living." We are the ones who grieve. Our loved ones on the other side are met with a great sense of peace, love, and wholeness when they cross over. Because of this, they are eager to comfort us so that we can go on living until we reunite with them again.

Once you open the door to the spirit, you can't close it!—Similar to the myth that we are always "on," there is nothing to fear regarding making a link to the spirit world. First, you are a spirit. You just happen to be encased in a physical shell. You are always in connection to the spirit world through your energetic systems. Therefore, you are never actually separate from the spirit world. What changes when you make a link with the spirit world is your awareness and focus, not your state of being. The modulator in your awareness of the spirit world is your attention and focus. When you are focused on the physical, you are more aware of the physical. When you are focused on the subtlety of energy, you are more aware of your spiritual or energetic body. This is how we become aware of the spirit realm. This is something that is temporary and cannot be maintained indefinitely because it requires energy and focus. Therefore, there is no situation where you would not be able to close the door on it. The default setting in the physical body is to not be aware of the spirit world. We get glimpses when we move our awareness there, but we are solidly grounded in the here and now.

Media-Based Myths

Mediumship has seen a transformation in its acceptance into the mainstream media. For a long time, mediumship was seen as something one did secretly with storefront psychics, and most would not share their experience with the public. The thought of visiting someone who "spoke to the dead" was seen as crazy or delusional. Thanks to mediums such as James Van Praagh, Sylvia Browne, and John Edward, mediumship was brought out of hiding and moved into the mainstream media in the 1990s and early 2000s.

James Van Praagh's *New York Times* bestselling book *Talking to Heaven* blew open the floodgates of interest in the unseen world and showed that, in the United States, people were hungry for this kind of information. With shows such as the *Montel Williams Show* hosting Sylvia Browne and *Crossing Over with John Edward*, mediumship was seen as a much more socially acceptable practice and met with more intrigue than derision.

Nowadays mediumship is everywhere—on TV, in countless books, in support groups, on social media, and more. With so much interest in the topic, ideas about what mediums are and how they conduct themselves vary greatly. This has led to a lot of misconceptions about what one should expect from a medium, how they experience the spirit world, and who can be a medium.

Unsolicited readings are a normal part of being a medium—Mediums are often portrayed in the media going to grocery stores, dentist appointments, and restaurants and giving messages to the unsuspecting store patron, dental assistant, and waiter. Conveniently, the television cameras were already rolling when the TV medium was struck at that moment with the sense of the spirit. While this makes great entertainment, it is far from the norm and—even more importantly—divorced from ethical mediumship.

It is important to recognize that the messages given on these shows are staged. While sometimes the actual readings are real, the circumstances are staged, the person getting the reading has already given consent and signed off on the appropriate forms, they are most likely getting some kind of payment, and they know exactly what is expected of them. Because of this, we should not view this kind of behavior as normal or ethical. These people on the shows have given their consent to be read. Going up to strangers in a grocery store and saying "I got ya motha here!" is wrong for many reasons, which I will discuss later in detail. For now, take the simple idea of consent as the basis of why this is inappropriate. Just as we do not go through a woman's purse without consent, we do not dig into other people's energy without consent. The medium should have permission from the recipient of the reading to read them. Also, the sitter must want a reading. Saying "I have a message for you from your dad if you want it" is also quite sketchy. If you find yourself doing this, ask yourself why and what it is giving you that makes you want to do this. More often than not, it is one's ego looking to be validated. No one needs to know you are a medium unless they ask or seek you out. Never force yourself on anyone.

Mediums always have to give a message—Related to the previous myth, mediums do not always have to give a message if they become aware of a spirit presence. It is often claimed by some mediums that they have to give the message for the sake of the spirit person. The reality is that even though we may become aware of a spirit's presence, it is up to the medium to decide how they should respond to it. We are never obliged to act on every impulse or impression that comes to us. In fact, often when I am aware of the presence of spirit, I will not engage it if it is not the appropriate time to do so. Spirit is with us all the time. They are always around to connect with. It is more likely our own awareness that happens to move into a sensitive state that tells us someone is there, not necessarily that the spirit is wanting to communicate. Remember, we are the ones in control of our mediumship, and unless it is the appropriate time and place with consent given, only then do we make a link to the other world out of respect for both medium and recipient.

Mediums have to use protection from negative spirits—The media has done an excellent job of making the unseen and the unknown terrifying for us. Horror films and books, combined with fear-based religious beliefs, make excellent fodder for thrilling entertainment for those wishing to be spooked. Movies like *The Conjuring, The Exorcist*, and more have created a belief in the frightening possibilities of connecting with unseen forces.

Even more damaging are the countless shows depicting real stories people have experienced and so-called paranormal "experts" citing demons, poltergeists, and all manner of dark entities as explanations for these experiences. These do very little in trying to bring understanding or clarity to what is actually going on with each person; rather, they only embellish and dramatize a fearful tale.

As a medium, it is my job to understand the spirit world as clearly and neutrally as possible. It is important for me to come to each connection to the spirit world with a grounded, evidence-based approach to clearly understand what the spirit is trying to bring me. In all my years of working with the spirit world, I have never experienced anything that led me to believe negative entities and spirits exist. Moreover, every teacher I have worked with, some being the most incredible mediums we have living today, also have never experienced any form of fearful interaction with the spirit world. It is for this reason that I know there is no need to protect myself from "negative" or "trickster" spirits. What I *have* encountered, however, is many people who misinterpret their experiences due to fear-based beliefs about the spirit world.

Crystals, sage, and diet will make you a better medium—Particularly popular amongst the New Age circles, the idea that external behaviors and rituals will make you a better medium is quite common. *Don't eat meat because it lowers your vibration. You can never have alcohol. Lapis lazuli will increase your psychic ability. Sage yourself after every reading.* Largely stemming from the lightworker movement in New Age spirituality, books have been written about how to eat and dress, what colors to wear, what thoughts to avoid, and an almost obsessive interest in one's vibrational state. These behaviors were thought to increase one's psychic and mediumistic abilities.

Fortunately, the reality is a lot simpler than this. There are no specific ways of living your life that will make you a better medium on their own. In fact, you can do away with all forms of restrictive ideas on how a medium should dress, eat, or think, or whether any of these things have any impact on your "vibration." The problem with these ideas is that there is no hard and fast rule to what and how a medium should be. What may be deleterious to one person's mediumship may not be for another. What is important is that you figure out what works best for you, your body, and your mind. If you are living an unhealthy lifestyle and it causes you to feel exhausted, moody, and unwell, you will be of no use to the spirit or others. Pay attention to what helps you. Moreover, if you find that burning something helps you get into the mediumistic headspace, by all means, burn away! But do know that it is not a requirement.

Your mediumship will only develop through training your awareness. This takes time, patience, and practice to get your mind to work in this sensitive way. A crystal, while beautiful, will not replace the personal and energetic work required to develop your mediumship. None of the above-mentioned rituals or practices will replace learning to cultivate stillness of the mind and passivity of awareness.

Mediumship is low vibration—Another common idea amongst the New Age lightworkers is that mediumship is somehow low vibration. The idea is that a medium must maintain a high vibration so that they can connect with the spirit world, which exists on a higher frequency of existence. While I would agree there is an energetic component to working with the spirit world, it is not something that we as mediums have to constantly strive to attain or change. One's energy is mostly affected by the way we feel. Therefore, you would only need to focus on the feeling of love, compassion, or harmony to "raise your vibration" to a state that will be conducive for spirit communication. Not only that, mediums learn to attune their awareness to their energetic senses and then wait for the power of spirit to move/inspire us into our connection. It is not something mediums have to create on their own. It is a partnership with spirit.

With all this talk of raising a vibration, it is funny to think that some people consider mediumship low vibration. The idea is that because a spirit presence incarnated, they are somehow behind in their development compared to those beings who have either transcended the human experience (ascended masters) or were never here to begin with (angels and otherworldly beings). In my experience, these labels that we put on spirit presences are just that—labels. They are an arbitrary, hierarchical way of making sense of the unseen world. For me, they are all the same thing, just presenting themselves differently. There is no real difference between them as they are just expressions of the divine. It is important to remember that your soul is eternal. It is not reduced to just the human form in this one lifetime. The divinity that exists in you now is the same divinity that exists in all of your being's lifetimes and expressions of evolution. To say that human souls are less divine shows a limited understanding of the nature of spirit and the soul. In this way, we understand that those who work with spirits of those who have crossed before us are not working with anything less than divinity expressing itself in an individualized form.

Mediumship is a closed practice (one must be born with it, be initiated into it, it's in one's culture/ancestry, etc.)—Mediumship is not unique to any one belief system or practice. Connecting with ancestors and those in the spirit world has been ubiquitous throughout time. Cultural and religious practices will vary from group to group, but the underlying experience is the same: connecting with those in spirit for guidance, remembrance, and respect for those who cross over before us.

Some systems of belief will require that a person seeking to connect with the spirit world be taught properly and pass through initiations or rituals prior to developing their spiritual gifts. While this is an appropriate measure for those who follow these specific lineages of spiritual practices, it is not a requirement for those who choose to develop their gifts outside of them. Also, some people believe that you must have a family member who was also a medium to be a true medium yourself. This is false. I have known many students who developed into incredible mediums without having any previous family members connected to this work. Each person and culture will have their own rules around communication with the spirit world, but know that even without them, mediumship is still possible and accessible to those who wish to connect to their loved ones in spirit. Mediumship is a natural part of who you are as a spiritual being. No belief system or rule can separate you from this awareness.

An Alternate Perspective on Negative Spiritual Experiences

Although we touched briefly on the concept of demons and evil spirits, I would like to take a closer look at this topic. As mentioned before, religious beliefs can be some of the most challenging beliefs to release ourselves from because we are often indoctrinated at a young age to fear the spirit world and the unknown. It is therefore important to explain to you why I know that there is nothing to fear from the spirit world—the least of which are things such as evil spirits, demons, curses, attachments, and possession. As we explore the topic of negative spiritual interactions, I hope to offer you an alternative perspective that might help to ease any fear around connecting to the world of spirit.

Evil and Negative Spirits

Let me begin by saying in my sixteen years of working with the spirit world, I have never experienced anything negative, scary, or bad. I have been to "haunted" places, house clearings, sites of great tragedy, and more, and nothing has ever followed me home, attached itself to me, or caused any form of harm. I have had unseen hands grab my arm, witnessed objects move across a space on their own, watched a table slide up a wall, and observed spirit lights moving around the space objectively. None of these experiences has ever caused me any kind of fear or unease. Why? Because knowing the mechanics of what makes spirit communication possible, even if there were negative entities wishing to do us harm, I know that no harm can come to us from those in the spirit world. But before we explore the mechanics/laws of spirit communication and why negative interaction with the spirit world is not possible, we need to understand a bit about human psychology.

Our belief systems play a huge role in how we perceive the world. All of our experiences have to pass through the lens and framework of these systems. Essentially, beliefs lead to perceptions, and perceptions lead to belief-confirming experiences. So when we have belief systems that are fear-based, our world becomes a lot scarier. We also are more likely to experience things that confirm these belief systems due to the way we interpret experiences we are having. A medium's beliefs about how the spirit world works will ultimately impact what and how we experience our mediumship. After all, all information coming from the spirit must pass through the mind of the medium. This is why it is so important for anyone who is wanting to develop their mediumship and receive clear, accurate, and specific information to learn how to set aside these fear-based beliefs so that they are able to become neutral about what they are experiencing. It is from a neutral place, not in fear or in fantasy, that we are able to accurately assess what is occurring in a given interaction with the unseen world.

For example, let us imagine I am making a link to the spirit world and I begin to feel a pressure on my neck that is quite firm. If I were a medium with a neutral, non-fear-based belief about connecting to the spirit world, I might feel this pressure on my neck and just describe it as such to my sitter—"I am feeling a firm pressure on my neck"—and then I would let this impression go and allow the next stimulus to occur. This next stimulus might make me aware that this spirit had trouble speaking at the end of their life. I would communicate this to my sitter and then move on with the reading. However, now let us imagine that I was a medium with a fear-based belief system and I began to feel a firm pressure on my neck. Believing that mischievous or evil spirits may try to attack me, I may start to question, "Is this something choking me?"

As soon as I have this thought, the sensation increases and my palms begin to sweat, my heart rate might rise, and my breathing may begin to become affected. As the new sensations occur, I may draw the conclusion a mischievous spirit is causing me to feel all these sensations. I begin to feel lightheaded and panic begins to set in. "I am under psychic attack!"

While both experiences begin with a firm pressure on the neck, one is able to notice the sensation, describe it, and then let it go, while the other may begin to react to the same stimulus with fear. The former medium will not react with fear regardless of any kind of sensation that occurs because they know that nothing negative can ever happen to them while connecting with spirit. They recognize the impression, even if slightly uncomfortable, is information meant to be passed to the sitter. The latter medium believes that protection is necessary from mischievous or negative spirits and that a medium must always be on their guard for their safety. A stimulus from a spirit that feels slightly uncomfortable could trigger a fear reaction and start an autonomic, or flight-or-fight, response. Especially when the source of the sensation is not clear, the unknown aspect adds to the fear. Also, if a medium has not learned how to notice, accept, and let go of any given stimulus, sometimes a strong sensation or feeling is hard to let go of because it is quite obvious to the medium. Because of this, once the fear and biological reactions start, it may be hard for the medium to know how to let go of what they are experiencing, thereby increasing the intensity or length of time of the uncomfortable stimulus.

Another example to illustrate this idea is let us say you are watching a sitcom in the living room of your house. You are laughing and enjoying yourself and then suddenly, out of nowhere, your roommate or partner comes into the room and asks "What are you watching?" Because you are in a relaxed and comfortable state, your reaction may be to laugh and tell them about how funny this show is. Now let us imagine you are in your living room, the lights are off, and you are watching a horror movie. The scene is leading up to the main character about to be caught.

Then, suddenly, out of nowhere, your roommate or partner comes into the room and asks "What are you watching?" It is very likely that in this instance, you would become startled, jump, and feel adrenaline pump through you. Notice that in both of these situations, the stimulus is exactly the same, but the perceived sense of danger greatly changes the reaction to an otherwise neutral experience.

Now that you understand how the mind and our belief systems can influence how we interpret stimuli coming from the spirit, let us look at why the mechanics of connecting to the spirit world do not support the ability of negative spirits affecting us, even if they did exist.

For spirit communication to work well, specific conditions are required of the medium, the space, and the participants. The spirit world requires energy to communicate with our side of life. After all, they are bridging dimensions of reality to connect with us. This is where the developed spiritual power of a medium comes into play. The spirit communicator will utilize the power of the medium to maintain a link with our side of life. As mentioned previously, the medium's energy is affected by what they feel. Imagine for a moment what you feel like when you are in love. The words that come to mind are openness, expansiveness, almost as though there is a welling up or overflow of loving feeling coming out from your heart. The overall concept is expansion of feeling. Now imagine when you are in fear; what is the first thing your body does? Your body contracts inward. Perhaps you cover your face, chest, or abdomen. The overall concept is a sense of drawing inward. Whether the outward expression of love or the inward pull of fear, our energy follows our thoughts and emotions. Therefore, when you are feeling loving, harmonious feelings, your energy expands; when you feel fear and tension, your energy contracts. This is important to understand as it relates to how we make a connection to the spirit world.

If we think of open energy as a means of saying "I'm open to connect with you" and closed energy as saying "I'm closed off to connecting," we can better understand the mechanics of making a link. When we want to make a link with the spirit world, we need to have an open and relaxed energy. This is because the spirit world utilizes our energy to maintain the link to our world, just as we use our open energy to link with theirs. They require a source of power, which is the power of our energy. The best way to achieve this is through the feeling of love, which naturally opens our energy. Also, a relaxed state of mind facilitates a receptive awareness and also opens our energy. Moreover, what we have been told from the spirit world, through mental mediumship and trance mediumship, is that mediumship works best in conditions that are friendly, loving, and harmonious. This produces conditions that are abundant with energy and ease. Your greatest links with the spirit world will always be marked by a strong sense of love and power. It is this concept of loving, open, relaxed energy that explains why negative spirits would not be able to affect our world.

As I mentioned before, the spirit world requires an energy source to make themselves felt and experienced in the physical world. Without this energy source, a link cannot be made. Therefore, if negative spirits did exist, they would not have power to negatively affect us in our world because there would not be enough energy available to them to do so. This is because as soon as they created any level of fear or tension in us, our energy would draw inward. When we are in a state of fear, our energy is not available to the spirit world because we are tense and closed off, thereby breaking the link. Mediumship requires freedom and relaxation to make our energy available enough to connect. If we are in fear, there is no way the spirit world can affect us or our awareness to become sensitive to their presence. Therefore, if you were in a situation where you were connecting with a spirit mediumistically and began to become afraid, you would lose the link very quickly. It is almost like a failsafe that keeps us separate.

You are safe and protected automatically by the very nature of how and why spirit communication works. This is not to say that those who have fearful experiences are not experiencing something; on the contrary,

I believe their experiences are very real and frightening. What I am saying is that the conclusion as to what is causing those experiences can be explained as psychological when put to the test. Maybe you yourself have had a scary or negative experience you have attributed to the spirit world. I would encourage you to revisit this experience and identify if there were any previous beliefs that may have contributed to the experience. I would also encourage you to set aside spirit consciousness as a possible source of the fearful experience and consider what else this could be coming from. Recognize that even in instances where people do not believe that spirits can harm or hurt you, the fear of the unknown or not understanding what is happening is strong enough to create all kinds of experiences.

Lastly, I would offer that in my experiences connecting to the spirit world, rather than finding fear, I have always been met with experiences of peace, love, harmony, friendship, support, and more. I have found that the more I connect with the spirit world, the more compassion and understanding is fostered in me. By learning to surrender and deepen my blending with my unseen helpers, guides, and Great Spirit, I have discovered a treasure trove of spiritual experiences that has changed my life for the better. The reality of spirit is subtle at first, but then it becomes far more magical and real than any story you have heard.

Possession and Exorcism

Possession is the idea that a spirit, generally negative, can enter the body of an individual against their will and cause harm to the host and those around them. Despite what religion and the media may want to portray, possession, especially against one's will, is not possible. This is because of the "one spirit, one body" rule of incarnation. You are the only soul that can be present in your body at all times. Even if you were to leave your body in an out-of-body experience or astral projection, nothing else can enter your body.

I can hear you saying, "But Michael, what about trance or channeling? Is this kind of like possession?" The answer is no. When a medium is moving into the trance state, the spirit's presence is not actually entering our body but rather blending their energetic aura with the medium's energetic aura. This can feel like the presence of the spirit is within them, but it is not—it is merely blended so well that it gives the experience of oneness with the spirit presence. Additionally, trance differs from possession in that possession implies being against the will of the individual. In trance we are welcoming and inviting the presence of spirit to draw near to us and utilize us for the purpose of spirit communication. It should also be noted that mediums have complete control of when this occurs and can end the session if they wanted to at any point. Our spirit friends are respectful of our space and time. It is a partnership with consent as its first rule.

Fear-based beliefs about the spirit world perpetuate the idea that possession is real. We also see this in modern times in many religious groups who claim to be casting out demons. As I have previously explained, we have nothing to fear from the spirit world, especially demons. However, this fear still pervades due to stories of possession.

One of the most famous movies to feature possession is *The Exorcist*. This movie is actually based on a real case of perceived possession of a young man, pseudonymously called "Roland Doe." I will share a summarized version of the way the story is often told to illustrate what I believe happens when fear-based beliefs are encouraged and what really is occurring when we see cases of "possession."

Spiritual or Psychological?

Before we move into the story of Roland Doe, I want to be clear that the feelings that come with perceived possession can feel very real, frightening, and overwhelming. I do not wish to negate the fact that these kinds of experiences can have a powerful impact on us physically and psychologically. Especially when we have others we consider an authority on spiritual matters reinforcing our perception, it can be quite traumatic and terrifying. In all instances of working with those who have had negative or scary experiences when trying to connect with spirit, I have found when offered an alternative perspective, great healing has come from the recognition that it was never the spirit world that was causing the fear or anxiety, but rather the interpretation of the events that created this. As we will discover below, the example described has more than one explanation—a supernatural one and a psychological one. I encourage those who have had a frightening encounter to suspend the supernatural explanation, revisit the memory, and consider the non-spiritual explanations. This way we can begin to explore what else may be the source of this experience and perhaps begin to heal our association with spirit and fear.

Roland was a thirteen-year-old boy in the late 1940s.[2] He had trouble in school and had behavioral problems. However, he was quite close to his aunt, who, conveniently enough, was a Spiritualist. She and Roland would use the Ouija board to communicate with the spirit world. Sadly, Roland's aunt passed away suddenly. This left him in great despair, and he was struggling. Shortly thereafter, Roland began to complain about knocks and raps he would hear in his room and that his bed would shake at night. Over time this escalated, and his parents contacted several experts in different fields, including psychiatrists, doctors, and their local Lutheran priest.

When nothing worked, they contacted a Catholic priest who believed that Roland was possessed due to strange occurrences that would happen only at night. The priest received permission to begin a series of

---

2   M. Opsasnick, *Part I: The Haunted Boy of Cottage City*, strangemag.com, http://www.strangemag.com/exorcistpage1.html (accessed January 17, 2022).

exorcisms on Roland, which only escalated the outbursts of behavior, including physical harm done to Roland's body by unseen forces. Following scratches that appeared on his body, Roland was moved to St. Louis, where a different group of priests continued the exorcisms. During this time Roland was strapped to beds, would react to sacred objects, and would speak in what seemed like Latin words. These occurrences happened every night for a month. Then, one evening, Roland was said to have seen a vision of Archangel Michael and was finally freed from his torment.

I share this story because it contains the hallmarks of what I believe occurs in cases of "possession." First, I should tell you that the supernatural and violent experiences that are often reported in relation to an exorcism are refuted by witnesses who were actually there. It is said that depending on who you spoke to, you got a different assessment of what was occurring. The psychiatrist would say Roland was mentally troubled, whereas the priests would say it was possession. Given what I know about the spirit world and what is often seen in cases of supposed possession, I have to assume the psychiatrists were correct.

In nearly every case that I have seen of reported possession, it almost always involves young teens or troubled individuals. If you were to read more in depth about the details of Roland's life at the time, it is evident that he suffered from some kind of behavioral issues. Add the stress and grief of the loss of his favorite aunt and it is a recipe for acting out or searching for attention. Whether consciously intentional or not, if you then give this child attention by adults who are showing care and concern for him, psychologically it is logical that he could be motivated to play into the belief of what was occurring. This is the danger of feeding this kind of belief: it can increase the behavior because now other adults are agreeing that it is real. This energy feeds itself and encourages it even without the presence of a malevolent spirit. Additionally, we often see possession in cases where there is already a belief that it is possible; you do not see it in cases where it is not believed to be so. We also tend to see possession claims in situations where a young person is in some kind of restrictive social system. Then, upon the acts of possession, they are able to express and behave in ways that they may otherwise not be allowed to.

Lastly, when behavior is labeled possession, there is a danger that the real issue, likely psychological in nature, is not being addressed. In this case, there was a grieving young man who was clearly troubled, as evidenced by the psychiatrists who evaluated him, who was then told by a spiritual authority figure that he had a malevolent force as the source of the issue. This only added to the problem and his actual issues were not addressed. It took a rather dramatic and cathartic experience to finally put an end to what was occurring.

It should also be mentioned that, in the case that there was actually some form of spirit involvement, particularly in the beginning with the raps and taps and even the shaking of the bed, were his Spiritualist aunt around, she would have been able to explain these phenomena and likely had a very different outcome. Any grounded Spiritualist would have been able to have given context to these experiences and likely dealt with what was actually happening rather than adding a fear interpretation into the mix. Granted, this is all speculation on my part. I do not know if there ever were actual spiritual rappings or movement of the bed. But if there were, these could have been addressed and understood from a non-fearful lens.

Using the story of Roland Doe, I hope you can take away that if we add fear-based beliefs to the mix, we are likely to have fearful experiences. The more we can move away from these beliefs, the less chance of misinterpreting these experiences as well as addressing the true issues that are at hand.

Curses and Attachments

If you have gotten this far, you can imagine what my thoughts might be on attachments and curses. The short of it is that they are not something you need to worry yourself about. That being said, let me explain why.

In my years of working as a psychic medium and in the spiritual field, I have had the unfortunate job of having to help people recover from other "mediums" and "psychics" who have told them that they are cursed. Many times my client had already spent thousands of dollars on a "cure" to erase this curse that was supposedly the cause of their poor love life, financial situation, or health. As evidenced by the fact they were coming to me, it is clear that this "cure" did not work.

To me, this kind of proclamation is one of the lowest of lows that someone claiming to be a psychic or medium can give. Those who push the idea of curses are usually the only ones who can see them. This is because it is a tactic to just take money and power away from the victims of these ploys. By saying "I see that you have a curse on you; for a fee, I will remove it for you," they are creating an issue that is not there and then saying they will cure you of it for money. It is an outright fraud. It is taking advantage of those in a vulnerable state who are seeking genuine help and support.

You will know that you are working with someone who is trying to scam you when they outright tell you you are cursed or they ask you to do a small ritual to solve your problem. Generally, the small ritual costs very little. Then they will reach out to you again and say that they need to do further work because it did not work the first time. This will usually cost more. They build up the fear and the issue more and more until you end up paying large sums of money for the solution you never needed. If you see this pattern at any time, stop it and get away as soon as you can from this person.

The issue I have with this is that curses have no power unless you believe in them, and that is not because of the curse actually being real but rather when we exist in the state of fear and the mindset that we are cursed, everything we experience will be blamed and placed on this. The "curse" is the belief that the curse is the cause of what is troubling people. This is a disempowering position and leaves us at the mercy of whomever told us we were cursed in the first place.

The reality is that we are in charge of our own energy and our experiences. While it may seem like an easy answer to point to something outside of myself and blame it, and with a couple prayers, candles, and ritual, our problems will be solved, it just is not real. Each of us must take personal responsibility for our lives and how they play out. Whether the issue is relational, financial, or something else, we need to see how we play into the issue. We may discover that we have a larger role than we previously imagined or we may discover that we need to let go of things that are no longer serving us, whether that is relationships, work, certain behaviors, or antiquated beliefs. These processes are often hard and uncomfortable. Recognize that life is not about pain aversion. In fact, we often have the biggest growth when we empower ourselves and decide to make change once and for all despite the challenge. I encourage you to recognize your own power over your life and energy. It is from this place that we have the power to rid ourselves of any "curse" we perceive in our lives.

Another very popular idea, especially amongst the New Age healers, is the idea of attachments. This is the idea that spirit presences can attach themselves to unsuspecting people and cause harm in their lives. They are usually pointed out in healing sessions or psychic readings as the cause or culprit in issues going on in someone's life. Generally, they will be perceived as a dark mass or entity in someone's auric field and can be removed by the person claiming you have them.

I have a bit more patience for the practitioner claiming attachments are present than when someone says a person is cursed. This is because, most times, they are only repeating what they were taught. By this I mean the practitioner may actually be picking up on something genuine in the energy of the client; however, they were taught that the meaning of this experience or stimulus is an entity or attachment. Because attachment and entity removal is often taught, those who learn from these teachers are never instructed any differently. Therefore, it is important to make a clear distinction between what an attachment really is versus what it is not.

Attachments are claimed to be spirit entities that attach themselves to an individual, often after some kind of trauma, abuse, or addiction, at some point in the client's life. These attachments are often removed by the practitioner through a combination of energy healing and processing verbally where this issue began, changing the client's experience or belief around it, and then releasing or removing it from the client's energy.

The reality is that the practitioner may genuinely be picking up on this kind of energy in the client's aura. However, the conclusion that this is a spirit entity is false. Spirits do not attach themselves to people. This would not be possible to maintain given the mechanics of mediumship I explained before and how spirit connections work between the spirit world and our world. Links with the spirit world and their impact on us are temporary and dependent on our ability to offer power and energy to them. This is a conscious and consenting process. As soon as the power runs out, so too does this link. Attachments have no consciousness within them. They are not spirit.

What is really happening is that the practitioner is picking up on some energetic buildup of energy in the client's aura and, because they were taught that this is what they were, erroneously conclude it is an entity with consciousness. The evidence that this is not consciousness is obvious when you consider how these "entities" are removed and resolved. This is done through psychological processing with the client and energetic movement of the built-up energy. Therefore, what attachments would more accurately be called are thought forms—strongly held beliefs or experiences that show up in the energy of an individual. Because our thoughts emanate out into our aura and energy, repeatedly played thoughts, patterns, behaviors, or beliefs can become obvious to those who are sensitive to the energy of others. These thought forms are there due to things like trauma, abuse, and strongly held beliefs.

Therefore, what is actually being removed and cleared are the energetic thoughts that are present in the individual's energy. This has nothing to do with spirit or consciousness of any kind.

Through a better understanding of what "attachments" really are, we have more power to address the actual issues someone is dealing with. By attributing our problems to some sort of unseen force outside of our control, we are disempowering ourselves and not addressing the true cause of suffering. Also, those who practice spirit entity removal are also disempowering their clients to take control of their own energy because they are essentially saying that the clients did not have the awareness that something was wrong, and now only the practitioner can clear it for them. This is taking the power away from the client and giving it to the practitioner. Helping clear energy and supporting others in processing their issues from their past is a positive thing; attributing it to an unseen spiritual force is not. As Gordon Smith always says, "No one is a victim of spirit." We should be teaching our clients how to manage and be aware of their own energy, empower their personal resolve, and encourage them to take control of their lives.

Myths About the Afterlife

We are all curious what happens after we die. There are countless answers to this question, along with differing cultural practices. In some belief systems, the disincarnate spirit enters a place of waiting, whether for redemption or temporary intermediary space; they are in some kind of holding pattern. In others, there is a journey that must be taken, filled with temptations, pitfalls, and challenges to reach the spirit world. There may be value in these beliefs and practices, not necessarily because it helps the spirit get to the other side but rather for those left behind. Often, in many traditions, there are rites to be said, prayers to be made, offerings to be given, and rituals to help lay the spirit to rest. These can last from days to months and even years. These practices are valuable in that they help communities grieve together. They allow those left behind something to do with their grief as death can often leave those of us left behind feeling powerless and directionless. Through coming together as a community and knowing what to "do" with death, we learn how to process and manage it.

With so many ideas about the afterlife, how can we know what it is truly like? We can consider near-death experiences as at least the beginning part of that process. Due to their consistent nature, we can catch a glimpse of some aspects of the journey—such as having clear awareness of the self, encountering some kind of being, a great sense of peace and love, and being drawn close to a point of crossing a point of no return. While the scope of near-death experiences is too great for this book, it does add some information to what we will likely experience as we make our way to the other side. For those of you who are interested in the scientific, empirical evidence for continuation of consciousness after bodily death, I recommend any work by Dr. Sam Parnia (see recommended resources), who is pioneering empirically based evidence of continuation of consciousness after clinical death.

I believe that, as mediums, we are privy to a part of that journey. I say *a part* because we are only given access to what we can experience through our mediumship. Therefore, there are some things we can know through the messages we receive. For example, there does seem to be some kind of recognition of the life they have lived and how their actions affected those around them in life. They seem to wish to make amends or right wrongs left over from their passing. They also seem to put a much larger emphasis on the relationships they made rather than the status they achieved or wealth they amassed. Our loved ones generally wish for us to know they are okay and that they are still here.

From the thousands of readings I have done, there are certain experiences of the afterlife that I have never heard any spirit person mention. These are some of the misconceptions or myths about the afterlife that I wish to clarify, largely because they tend to create great pain and strife for those left behind in addition to the grief they are already experiencing from their loss. While you may hold some of these beliefs, I hope to offer you an alternative perspective so that you might best support those in grief. Also, it is a great opportunity to consider where the mind and the ego may be entering into one's mediumship and beliefs.

Being Stuck or Lost

In my years of working with the spirit world and providing countless numbers of very specific and accurate readings, I have never come across a spirit who did not know they were dead, who was stuck, or who needed my help to get to the other side. My experience has been that all spirit people get to the spirit world. This is because it is not an option to remain here attached to the physical plane of existence, nor is it an option to remain in the "astral realm." When our time here ends, our connection to the earthly plane ends, and our awareness moves to a higher, more expanded, timeless space. You are already connected to this state of awareness at this very moment. The only difference is that your brain is acting as a condenser of consciousness so that you can be here and live a physical life. When the body dies, your consciousness merely expands and refocuses into your spiritual being and awareness. There is no wandering, stuckness, or needing to get somewhere else.

The idea of a spirit being lost is due to our understanding of the physical world. We see it as our individualized self needing to find our way in the vast unknown. The reality is, we are already connected to the spirit world. Also, we have spirit helpers whom we know meet us along our journey to welcome us back to this greater connection. If when we passed we could get lost, what would our guides be good for if not to guide us to the spirit world? It is so important to clear up this myth because I have seen it do terrible things to those who are grieving. Not only are they dealing with the loss of their loved one, but now they are also concerned that their loved one is lost in some unknown spiritual realm. It is just harmful and unhelpful in every way. Not only is it not true, but I do not see any value in telling someone this. It seems to just be in cases where the "medium" is saying something to the effect of "Your loved one is lost, but I will help them cross to the light." In my experience of those who do this kind of thing, they generally are not very evidential in their work or their minds are quite active in the work that they do. I implore anyone who does say these things to consider the damage that may be occurring to those who hear it and recognize that there are alternative perspectives one can try on that do not cause this kind of pain.

Rescue Circles

Related to the previous example, rescue circles are spirit circles that exist to help spirits who are stuck or lost cross over. As mentioned previously, it is my experience that no spirit is ever stuck or lost. In the rescue circles I have attended, I am left wanting for any real evidence to validate the existence of the communicator. In instances where evidence is provided, the spirit communicator was invariably connected with one of the rescue circle members. This would be no different from a normal spirit message except for the end portion where they are asked to go into the light. More often I have seen messages come through that cannot be validated until the medium returns the following week with someone who fits the description found in a google search. Mediumship should always be evidential and show the intelligence of the spirit world at work. To make a connection with someone who has no relationship to the spirit's relatives, friends, or even country would not show a purpose or meaning to why the spirit is wanting to connect. Evidenceless messages can be an easy trap for the ego. They can make people have a sense that they are connecting and doing good with the idea that they are helping those lost souls cross over. But without solid evidence to support this, we cannot accept the claims of crossing spirits over as fact. However, I do not disregard these circles completely.

I do believe that in some cases there can be some kind of good being done in these circles. Instead of viewing the circle as crossing over loved ones but rather as clearing away the "stain" of the emotional or mental energetic trauma around a passing, I think there may be some kind of value found. Whenever something traumatic happens, it makes an impact on the atmosphere around where it occurred. Perhaps, in some instances, these circles are working to remove the painful memory or unresolved trauma energetically.

Suicide

The myth that suicide deaths are somehow treated differently than any other kind of passing is the most common of myths I encounter. The belief is that because someone dies by suicide, they have somehow needed to enter a time of rehabilitation, a purgatory state, or in some way be punished for this action. I cannot stress enough how untrue this is. There is no difference in experience for anyone who dies by suicide compared to dying by any other mode. The reality is that a death is a death regardless of how it happens. I say this not to diminish the tragic pain and loss, but rather to remove the judgment around deaths by suicide. There is no cosmic judgment that befalls someone due to crossing over this way. I have easily connected with countless loved ones in spirit who passed to the otherworld in this way. They are often eager to communicate to bring comfort and understanding to those still left behind.

I believe that the source of this myth stems both from religious belief and also judgment that is consciously or unconsciously placed on those who cross over through suicide. Many people have strong feelings of discomfort or judgment, as evidenced by phrases such as "That was so selfish" or "How could they leave their child behind?" While the emotions of hurt or loss are valid, the judgment might not be. Consider that those who do choose to end their own lives are more in need of our compassion and understanding. In most instances, these individuals struggled greatly in their lives. They often have years of mental health issues, chronic physical health issues, and more, which often go unheard or treated. We have to change the way we look at death by suicide. Instead of judgment, understand that this person chose to end their personal suffering. We must realize that we will all make this crossing at some point, and while I personally would want everyone to make it to a happy, healthy old age, this will not be the case for everyone. Death is not an ending but an event in the life of an individual. The more we recognize this, the more we may come to not judge how one passes.

2

Understanding the Authentic Medium's Experience

On the journey of your development, you will likely be gifted with many beautiful moments of insight and amazement—and also have your ego and traumas triggered. This is all part of the medium's journey. Our goal is to do our best to celebrate our wins and learn from our challenges. Obstacles to genuine spiritual connection will always show up; however, by having an awareness of what to expect, we can learn to mitigate these moments and quickly find our way back to true genuine connection. This chapter will provide you with important tools and definitions to aid you in your spiritual awareness as well as understanding how to stay authentic by avoiding unnecessary potential pitfalls.

What to Expect on Your Mediumship Journey

Having taught for many years now and having had the pleasure of watching mediums develop from the beginning of their journey—with no awareness of the spirit world—to advancing to fully fledged working mediums, there seems to be commonality in the highs and lows a medium's journey takes. With this in mind, it is important that I share some of these common experiences in hopes to manage expectations as you unfold on your journey. Hopefully this information will encourage you to continue your journey and help you know that it is completely normal when you experience these highs and lows.

Generally speaking, during the beginning of one's discovery of their mediumistic abilities, the budding medium is excited, enthusiastic, and mind blown that spirit communication is real. Often students feel like they have finally found their purpose and their calling in life. They can feel vindicated about past experiences that left them confused or outcast and often experience a sense that their lives make sense for the first time. As they delve deeper into this journey, they are eagerly soaking up every bit of information: YouTube binges, hundreds of books (probably this one included!), and hours of workshops and classes fill this time. A budding medium is all excitement and wonder. It is an incredible time of personal discovery and what feels like fast spiritual growth. Assuming that they have some success in the beginning of their development, a fledgling medium will begin to learn to trust themselves and their spiritual experiences. This time period often lasts several months to a year.

As a medium begins to feel more confident in their ability, they begin to enter a stage I refer to as "having enough information to be dangerous." This is the time period where a medium has soaked up incredible amounts of information combined with a small amount of personal experience. They may be still insecure in their work but confident in their understanding of how it all works. For some reason, invariably, the newish medium often feels the need to become a substitute teacher to those who are just a bit behind them in their development. The challenge with this time period is that they are still full of enthusiasm but do not have enough experience to necessarily support the information they often try to teach others. This is why I say they have enough information to be dangerous. This is generally where the ego of the medium begins to develop and rear its head. This is also the time period where some students decide they know enough to work with the public or even begin teaching themselves.

I have to take a moment here to stress the importance of taking your time in your development before working professionally. While I can understand the passion and enthusiasm to get out there and begin helping people with your newfound ability, what is often lost on new mediums is that mediumship is about far more than giving a message successfully. It is about the cultivation of the whole medium. We are working with people who are in varying stages of grief, and it is important that a medium has experienced the gamut of potential hiccups, challenges, and situations in their readings so that they know how to best support someone in this delicate state. Not only that, but what a medium says and does has a lasting impact on a sitter in this state of mind. Were the reading to go awry, it could cause lasting hurt to the sitter.

There is a strange phenomena that occurs in the power dynamics of a reader and a sitter. For some reason, when a medium says, "I have information from a supernatural source," the subconscious mind of the sitter, whether they believe in mediums or not, opens up and takes the information to heart. Even if the sitter doesn't believe in mediums, somewhere in the back of their mind they will always remember what was said and think, "Remember that medium once said…" This is why it is so important we are careful with what we tell a sitter.

Additionally, a developed medium has awareness and understanding of their connection to spirit and their own limits and abilities. Far too often, underdeveloped mediums try to be the solution for all problems faced by the sitter. For example, a developing medium may try to provide psychological assessments when they have no training or accreditation ("You don't need to be on your medications" or "Your husband is a narcissist"). They may try to diagnose an issue or provide remedies outside of their expertise ("Colonics will cure your problems"). We must be realistic and grounded in knowing what we can and cannot do for our sitter. Lastly, information has very little value until it is backed by experience. While one can have knowledge, it is experience that turns it into wisdom. Time and time again, I have students who wish to forge ahead full speed with their mediumship and get up on a public platform or do readings for the public. They come to me and ask if I think they are ready. While it is not up to someone else to tell you when you are ready to work publicly, an experienced teacher can give you a sense of where you are at in your journey based on their knowledge of the medium's journey. When these students come to me, I give them my honest assessment and will often encourage them to wait for a specific period of time. Every time I have done this with a student and they have listened, they have later thanked me for telling them to wait because some breakthrough in their understanding had occurred that was necessary for their mediumship to flourish.

Development of your mediumship is not linear. You will have time periods where your mediumship is on a high, where every reading is effortless and you are jumping from strength to strength. There will be other times where you may be asking yourself if you can even do this work. Your mediumship will work one way for a time, perhaps all pictures and feelings, and then suddenly change and not work at all how it used to. This can be very concerning for many students. This is completely normal. The ebbs and flows of one's mediumistic journey are natural. As we change, so too does our mediumship. Also, the spirit world is trying to cultivate a multimedium—someone who can experience their spiritual gifts in a multitude of ways. Learn to move with whatever time period you are in. When you are experiencing the highs, relish it, enjoy it, and know that you are moving forward in your work. When things are feeling stuck, slow, or not working as they once did, recognize that this is merely an ebb season. Frequently, this time period coincides with other areas of your life that require your attention. Whether that is personal, relational, or another way, there is likely stress in your life that is causing tension in your mediumship. Take time to reflect and notice what other areas of your life require your attention. Once these issues are resolved, your mediumship will likely return to normal.

It is also important to recognize that mediumship generally grows slowly over time. Sure, in the beginning there can be huge leaps in your work. However, this tends to settle down, and a much slower pace takes its place. You may think you have plateaued for a time period and then all of a sudden you start to become aware of new types of information or perhaps you begin to become aware of greater detail than you had before. Things that once seemed hard become standard in your messages. A perfect example of this in my own journey was getting excited if I could feel if the spirit communicator was a male or female—sounds basic and simple, but at one point this was very challenging for me. Now this is a completely effortless awareness, and my new excitement is when I am given the street address of where the spirit person once lived or words in other languages I have never heard of before. But this kind of growth doesn't happen overnight. It is the tiny bits of growth that add up over time. These tiny jumps in your growth are like tiny grains of sand, often going unnoticed. Eventually you look back and there is an entire sandy beach behind you. So be patient with your development and never compare what you are doing now to what someone else is accomplishing who has far more experience than you. You were not present for the time of dedication, the countless noes, and tiny jumps in growth along the way. You are seeing the end product of years of work. Take your time— there is no rush—and enjoy the journey. That is the most important part of all.

Working with the Power

If you want to grow in your spiritual awareness, I cannot stress enough the importance of understanding and working with "the power." It is one of the most important and powerful discoveries in my development as a medium. The power is the felt presence of spiritual energy that precedes any form of spirit connection, communication, or phenomena. It is often experienced as a change in atmosphere that is highly palpable. For some reason, in American mediumship it is not commonly discussed and rarely taught. So it wasn't until years into my development that I began understanding this vitally important force as the foundation of mediumship that it is.

Chapter 2

Many new mediums find it hard to know what the power is until they experience it fully for themselves. As my mentor Eileen Davies always said, "Power is a lot like love. It is hard to describe or understand until you've experienced it yourself." For those with a Christian background, I often use the example of the Holy Spirit as a comparable descriptor of how the power works. Several times in the Christian Bible, there are references to the Holy Spirit descending upon individuals like a dove and then some kind of miracle occurring. I believe this is the exact experience that mediums have, only we call it something different.

Although it may be hard to recognize at first, many mediums will already be working in the power and just not recognize this is what they were experiencing. So what does the power feel like and how do you know you're in it? What makes it hard to recognize is that each person experiences the power slightly differently. Even more confusing, depending on the type of mediumship that is being practiced (something we'll get into in the next chapter), the power will feel differently. Even so, the commonality is that the power is a felt experience. It is experienced through our clairsentience as different sensations such as pressure on the back of the neck; thickening, heaviness, or electrification of the atmosphere around you; a sense of ramping up or subduing internally; or temperature changes such as hot flashes or cool breezes. There can also be a change to your awareness such as heightened awareness or alertness, feeling dissociated or "out of it," sleepiness, or feeling subdued. However it is felt, the experience of your awareness and energy moving from its normal state to an altered state is the indicator that you are moving into the power.

In the beginning of their development, students often feel like it is up to them to somehow guess at or try to gather the information coming from spirit. What I try to help them to recognize early on is that mediumship does not come from our mind but rather from the power. All we are doing in mediumship is becoming sensitive, sensing the power, and describing how we are energetically changing from moment to moment.

The source of this energetic change comes from the power. Therefore, the more we can learn to blend and work in the power, the less we will try to search for information and instead let it come to us through the natural flow of the energy around us. Mediumship happens to us, not from us.

We'll get more into working with the power in part 4 when we dive into step-by-step guidance for developing your mediumistic abilities.

The Clairs

As you grow in your spiritual awareness, you will begin to develop your spiritual senses. Just as we experience the world through our physical senses of sight, hearing, taste, smell, and touch, so too do we have similar senses through which we experience the spirit world and energy. We call these the "four clairs." The four clairs are clairvoyance, clairaudience, clairsentience, and claircognizance. *Clair* is a French word meaning "clear." Therefore, each one of the clairs represents a "clear" sense we use to experience energy and spirit. Clairvoyance is sight, clairaudience is hearing, clairsentience is feeling, and claircognizance is knowing. Together, these four clairs are used by the spirit world to deliver impressions to us to convey their messages.

Clairvoyance

Clairvoyance is likely the most recognized of the clairs as it has often been used as a standalone phrase to mean "a medium" or "a sensitive." However, as it relates to the clairs, *clairvoyance* means "clear seeing." This is the spiritual faculty we use to "see" spirit and energy. There are two types of clairvoyance: subjective and objective. Subjective clairvoyance is the most common. This is the experience of seeing spirit or energy through the mind's eye. It is experienced as a flash of an image, not unlike the way we recall the memory of an image. Some clairvoyants can also see movie-like vignettes play out in their mind. Objective clairvoyance is much more rare. This is where the sensitive can see spirit or energy with their physical eyes. For objective clairvoyants, it may be difficult to distinguish between what is real in the physical world from what is coming from the spirit. Neither way of experiencing clairvoyance is better than the other.

Mediums use clairvoyance to see information such as physical descriptions of the spirit communicator, specific words or phrases wishing to be passed on, visuals of shared memories, important physical objects, places, and much more.

Clairaudience

Clairaudience means "clear hearing," and it is how we perceive sounds from the spirit world. Clairaudience is easily one of my favorite clairs due to its accuracy and efficiency. Essentially, all a clairaudient has to do is repeat what they hear, exactly as they hear it, and it will be correct. Almost all of the most incredible mediums we have ever had were clairaudient, which makes sense. Clairaudience is used by the spirit to relay all manner of information including full names, dates, names of places, songs that were relevant to the communicator, and sounds connected to the spirit such as keys jingling or coins rattling in the pocket. Whatever sounds are significant to the spirit communicator can be conveyed. Clairaudience is often experienced as a flash of sound that occurs without looking for it. It can be experienced outside of the body or inside. It may or may not sound like your own voice.

For me, clairaudience often sounds like a whisper over my shoulder or within an inch or so of my head. However, clairaudience does not have to be localized around the ears or head. Some mediums of the past heard the sound in their solar plexus. Sounds can occur anywhere within the medium's energy.

Clairsentience

Clairsentience means "clear feeling." For me, it is the most important of the clairs. As my mentor Gordon Smith always said, "Mediumship is the art of feeling." I couldn't agree more. Clairsentience allows us to feel the presence of spirit when we are communicating with them. It lets us know when they draw near, which takes the guesswork out of knowing when spirit is near us. Clairsentience is also how we experience the power. Clairsentience can be experienced as tingling, buzzing, warmth, heaviness, thickness in the atmosphere, pressure on the body, and any other physical sensations we experience. It can also be experienced as emotion and inspiration from within us. Through this sense of feeling, we are able to feel the presence of spirit, sense their emotions, and feel the size and shape of our communicator. Clairsentience is also important because any other clair that we receive information through will almost always have a clairsentient component to it. Clairsentience provides context to what we are experiencing.

People often cite *clairgustance* (clear tasting) and *clairolfactory* (clear smelling) as separate clairs; however, I consider these a part of clairsentience since they are being experienced through a physical stimulus upon the body.

Claircognizance

Claircognizance is considered a newer addition to the clairs. This is the sense of "clear knowing." This sense is experienced as information landing in your awareness seemingly without a specific stimulus to indicate how you have perceived it. This is often experienced as a burst of inspiration in your awareness or as if you already know something to be true all of a sudden. All manner of information can be gleaned through claircognizance because it is awareness of information as fact, without any need for interpretation or understanding. It just is.

Psychism vs. Mediumship

Utilizing our clairs allows us to access information that is not gleaned through physical means. These include both psychic and mediumistic impressions. I am often asked what the difference is between a psychic and a medium. This can be a confusing distinction to make given that in our culture today, the term *medium* is often used interchangeably with the term *psychic*. There are many similarities between psychics and mediums. They both use the four clairs to get their information. Both psychics and mediums can sense the subtle energies around a person. Both can get information about your life and even information about your loved ones. However, the difference between a psychic and a medium is the source of the information they perceive and where they focus their awareness. A psychic will focus their awareness on the energy of the client, an object, a specific physical location, or the energy around a specific situation and often become aware of past, present, and future events and information. Moreover, a psychic can become aware of what is happening physically, mentally, emotionally, or spiritually with their client.

How does this differ from a medium? A medium most likely can become aware of the same kind of information as a psychic, but there is an old saying that "All mediums are psychic, but not all psychics are mediums." This means that while a psychic uses their awareness to tune into the energy of people, places, objects, and events, they may not necessarily become aware of the presence of spirit people. This is because the psychic may not have been trained in how to make and hold a link with the spirit world.

A medium can be thought of as a telephone to the spirit world. They focus their psychic senses (the four clairs) on the spirit world and become aware of the loved ones who have crossed over who wish to communicate with their loved one here on earth. A medium spends their development learning how to make a link with a spirit communicator, hold it, and pass on information to provide evidence of the survival of consciousness. A good medium should be able to provide evidence that will help you recognize which of your loved ones they are connecting with. This can include personality traits, relationship to the client, names or important dates, shared memories, physical descriptions, and more. Once the identity is sufficiently established, then a message from that loved one in spirit can be brought forward. A psychic could bring through information about your loved ones who have crossed over; however, they would be describing this person through what they perceive in your energy. They would be describing the energetic signature that is in your energy about your loved one, but there would not be the actual presence of your loved one in spirit. While both mediums and psychics use their psychic senses, only a medium can bring through the presence of your loved ones in spirit. Neither psychicsm or mediumship is better than the other; it just depends on what kinds of information you're looking for. They are just two different ways of accessing information.

Many mediumship purists will often say that psychism and mediumship should not be used together—either you work psychically or mediumistically in a reading. I do not agree with this sentiment. Sure, a medium does need to be developed and trained on how to get just psychic information or just mediumistic information. Being able to differentiate is important because if a sitter comes to you looking for a mediumship reading and all you provide is psychic information, they will leave disappointed. Conversely, if your sitter is coming to you to get guidance on their current life situation, you would not want to spend the reading talking about their grandmother and the memories they shared. For the purpose of training and development, working just psychically or just mediumistically is important. However, once the skill of working solely psychically or mediumistically is well developed, it is no longer necessary that a medium work exclusively one way. I believe that as long as there is healing occurring in the reading, if we hand the reading over to the spirit world, the right information will occur. The spirit world knows better than we do what is needed for the sitter. If that means we give some mediumistic information and some psychic information, so be it. The spirit world knows best.

Remaining Grounded for
Genuine Spiritual Connection

In time, as we become more skilled in our advancing spiritual awareness, it will become even more important to remain grounded, accurate, practical, and truthful in our approach to our spiritual work,
whether it be psychic or mediumistic. To this end, I think it is important
to highlight common potential pitfalls I have seen as one develops their
mediumship and spiritual identity.

For the last twenty-five-plus years, the label of "lightworkers" has
been emphasized in the New Age spiritual scene. Along with it has been
an influx of emphasis on the "light" and making sure one's vibration is
high enough and spiritual enough. Often associated with this work are
angels and ascended masters, significant numbers, crystals, and different
types of "earth angels." While there is no harm in being a lightworker,
I believe it is important to recognize that all spiritual work should come
from a grounded, practical approach to reality.

Misleading Behaviors

It is far too easy to get lost in the clouds of über-spirituality. It is not eating the right thing, wearing the right colors, or adorning yourself with
crystals and sage that will make you more spiritual or more intuitive. In
fact, it is often these behaviors that tend to keep people from going into
the depth of their spiritual journey. This is because when we believe that
wearing certain crystals or eating a specific way will somehow boost our
"consciousness," we are often not taking the time to learn to become
still, quiet, and present. These spiritual accoutrements are easy ways to
"feel" spiritual without having to do the slow, dedicated work to develop
one's awareness. I say this because I spent many years of my development attempting to unfold my gifts in this way. While they were fun
and they felt good, it truly only cultivated imagination and fantasy, not
the reality of genuine spiritual connection. I know I am not alone in this
experience because whenever I have taught students who were coming

from this orientation, they have always expressed to me how "real" the spirit world became after dispensing with anything extra and realizing that everything we have is already within us. We just have to work at it.

Addressing Toxic Positivity

I also think it is important to recognize that one of the greatest dangers of the "love and light" and "high vibes only" attitude often associated with the lightworker's way can lead us into spiritual bypassing. Spiritual bypassing is when an individual uses spiritual practices or ideas to avoid dealing with personal issues, psychological traumas, and underdeveloped parts of oneself. By having the "positive vibes, love and light only" motto, we are often never dealing with the harsh, uncomfortable, and real issues happening around us.

No, having a negative thought will not manifest it into your life. Dealing with the painful past will not manifest it into your future. Being frustrated or angry about something will not make you diminished in any way. If anything, suppressing and ignoring your true needs or feelings will! This creates tension, and as we have learned thus far, it has a deleterious effect on your spiritual awareness. There is nothing positive that comes from only being positive all the time.

This is not to say one needs to wallow in their pain and their grief, but it is important to deal with what is real. The more we deal with ourselves and truly work to heal and grow through the challenges life throws at us, the more we will evolve. This is vitally important, particularly in mediumship. You need to be able to be a rock for those who are in need of support. If you are uncomfortable with your own pain, how can you expect to be of any support to others? Moreover, going through the ups and downs of life strengthens us, teaches us, and widens our experience so that we can reach deeper into supporting others.

Empaths

Often associated with lightworkers, the identification as an empath is very common. Empaths are generally defined as people who are very sensitive. A quick internet search of *empath* will usually bring up a list of criteria that you just might be one. These include things like a natural caregiver; sensitive to sounds, people, places, and crowds; poor boundaries; love of nature; and needing time by yourself to recharge. Personally, by this definition, nearly every person in my life is an empath. Not only that, definitely every student I have is an empath as well. I believe that it is important to not make being an empath something overly special or unique because people tend to tie it to their ego and their identity. By doing this, we often see self-proclaimed empaths as always needing to remind everyone that they are so sensitive, that the world is too much, and that they are incredibly intuitive, picking up on everything. Now don't get me wrong: these things can be challenging. Being sensitive really can be tricky because the world really can be overwhelming. I can speak to that very much. However, that does not mean I am a victim to my circumstances. It is important, then, for me to explain what I feel the true power of an empath is and how we can use it to become empowered in one's sensitivity, not a victim to it.

When someone claims that they are an empath, there seems to be an implied point being made: that they are "too sensitive" for everything and are picking up on too much—and this may be true. However, I think viewing empaths this way leaves them at the mercy of circumstance and environment. Whether loud or aggressive people, crowded places, or any other uncomfortable circumstance, empaths are left to just manage their discomfort without any power to change the atmosphere around them. Why is it that an empath must always receive? Therefore, I always try to teach my empathic students that the real power of an empath is to *feel*.

Before we jump into what I mean by this, it is important to understand how energy and feelings work. Imagine for a moment that you walk into a room after a couple has just been fighting. You can sense that there was an argument or a fight because the air feels charged—there is a sense of tension and discomfort. This is you picking up on the energy of the space. Why? Because space is not just air; it is better to think of it as a fabric that can be imprinted upon. In all places, objects, and spaces, we can affect the space around us through imprinting the space. As another example, imagine a holy place or site that people have visited with great reverence and sacredness. This space has a very specific feeling whether people are there or not. Why? Because people have gone there for ages and *felt* the feeling in the space. In a way, you can think of this as people having "stained" the space with whatever feeling that has been expressed over and over again.

Why is this important to understanding empaths? It is important because the gift of an empath isn't just to feel others' emotions or environments around them but to exude feeling as well. Empaths have the gift of feeling deeply and strongly. It is this ability to feel deeply and strongly that puts out a great strength and power of feeling, which will have a great impact in "staining" the atmosphere around them. So really, an empath has a *greater* ability to affect the space around them than not. How, you might ask? By building up their own energy and exuding how they want others to feel into the space.

To build up your energy, I recommend sitting in the power, which is a practice you will learn later on in chapter 8. However, you can also learn to do this by first recognizing what is your energy and becoming present in your own space. You are allowed to take up space; your opinion matters; your desires are important; they do not come second to anyone else. It is this kind of mentality that will help build up your own energy. Empaths have often experienced a lot of trauma in their younger years with reactive or explosive parents. Because of this, they have learned to sense and feel the atmosphere around them constantly, looking for the next danger or the next problem. It is important for an empath to learn how to be present in their own space and learn to hold it. Then, once they have learned how to take up some space, they can fill that space with whatever they want to feel around them—and not just for them but what they want others to feel as well.

As I mentioned before, to affect a space, we need to feel the emotions we want to imbue the space with. You can think of things like peace, love, harmony, joy, etc. We need to not just think about these feelings but actually feel them in a real and experiential way. This helps express the energy of this emotion out into the energy around you. The more we learn to hold this emotionally balanced and peaceful state, the more you will affect others with it. A perfect example of what you are creating is to think of someone you know that when you are around them, you feel calmer, at peace, and much safer in their energy. Just by being in their presence, others feel more at ease. This is what you are learning to cultivate. This way you are not at the mercy of the feelings in the environment around you, and you can actually change the energy and attitude of those you interact with. At the very least, you will be holding a barrier around yourself filled with how you want to feel.

This isn't something you have to consciously be thinking to hold. That would be exhausting. What you want to do is practice this process regularly so that it becomes a default or natural state of being. This may require you to do some inner work as well, so do not shy away from that. If you have a hard time feeling empowered or valuable, this is a great place to start. Through understanding what the true power of an empath is, we can learn to take control of our environment and how we feel as well as gain a much-needed sense of boundaries and the self. We will no longer be at the mercy of circumstance and be reactive or affected by whatever way the wind is blowing. You have great power, my empath friends; let's move from victimhood to empowerment.

Avoiding Cold Reading, Hot Reading, and Mentalism

I would be remiss if I did not discuss a point most skeptics will often allege against you. Not only is it important to know to prevent skeptics from claiming you are a fraud, but also so that you do not find yourself accidentally doing it. This is the topic of cold reading, hot reading, and mentalism. It will help the developing medium to understand what these are and how to avoid them.

Cold Reading

In general, this is what you will most likely be accused of by the skeptic. Cold reading is the tactic used by fraudulent mediums or psychics to gather information by using highly probable, vague, or general questions or statements to elicit a response from your sitter that will quickly tell the reader if they are giving the right information or not. Essentially, the reader will use other subtle cues like facial expressions, reactions, and verbal or nonverbal cues to guess the correct information. This is often done through asking questions and then saying, "Oh yes, because I was getting…"

A genuine medium will not be cold reading. In fact, it is likely harder for a genuine medium to try to use cues from the sitter because it distracts from the connection to the spirit communicator. This does not mean it cannot accidentally happen. For the under-trained medium, oftentimes the facial expressions or how something is responded to can give a clue or a hint if one is giving correct information or not. This is why it is important for the medium to develop indifference to the sitter, and the less the sitter says, the better. This is why I develop my students to only have their sitters say *yes, no, I don't know,* or *I need more information,* validating information the medium is giving. Also, the medium should not be asking questions of the sitter except for "Does this make sense to you?" Mediums should be making statements throughout a reading.

Unfortunately, many mediums with great potential are not trained this way and have been taught to ask questions of the sitter. It is vitally important to learn to get information without asking questions, just making statements and getting as little information from your sitter as possible. Then, as you get better, it will actually become easier and easier to get information. In fact, the less you know will be easier than knowing anything about your sitter. To me, the less I know, see, and hear, the better!

Hot Reading

Hot reading is not something that can be done accidentally, so as long as you are not committing outright fraud, you will not have to worry about doing this one. Hot reading is when the reader already knows information about the sitter without the sitter knowing. They then provide this information as psychic or mediumistic information.

This is outright fraud if done with intent to deceive or appear more accurate than you are. This is different from knowing something from a previous conversation or interaction and telling your sitter, "Hey, I remember this from our conversation" or "You already mentioned this, but I am getting…" In those instances, you are clarifying with your sitter that this is previous knowledge you had and making it clear it is not coming from the spirit world or psychically. It is so important to do this to avoid hot reading. Hot reading is fraud, plain and simple. Do not ever look up anything about your sitter. It is bad for you, them, the spirit, and psychism and mediumship in general. It is more noble to get it wrong or get nothing.

Mentalism

Mentalism is performed by a mentalist, who is someone that has learned to gather information about a person through reading body language, subliminal communication, emotional intelligence, and an understanding of psychology and human behavior. In general, they are attempting to appear like they are getting the information supernaturally, though they will admit that they are not. Mentalists often are trying to dissuade people from seeing psychics or mediums because they believe this is how they are getting their information.

A genuinely developed medium is not a mentalist. They do not need bodily cues, subliminal communication, or even an understanding of human behavior to give clear, accurate, and specific information. This is evidenced by the many studies that have been done to debunk this claim. The Windbridge Research Center, headed by Julie Beischel, has devised a quintuplet blind study[3] that completely rules out mentalism or any form of cold reading. Through this, she has effectively shown that mediums are gathering information from some other supernatural means. In my own training, and how I train my students, we often do blind or proxy readings. In blind readings students do not know who they are reading and are not getting any feedback until the end. In proxy sittings you have someone else sit in as the sitter, but the intent is to read someone else; then the reading is scored afterward by the person the reading was intended for. This rules out any kind of mentalism.

Authenticity is paramount to cultivating a true and genuine medium-istic ability. Without it, we fall victim to our egos, with our minds contaminating our messages from spirit, at worst resulting in fraudulent behaviors. By exploring what the authentic medium's developmental experience is like, we can avoid many of the pitfalls and ego traps that can come along the journey. Moreover, we are able to stand strong in the authenticity and accuracy of our work with the spirit world. Be patient in your development, and understand that dedication to your spiritual progress over time is the key to unfolding the highest potential of your mediumship.

---

3   J. Beischel, *Completed Studies—Windbridge Research Center*, Windbridge.org, https://www.windbridge.org/research/completed-studies/ (accessed January 17, 2022).

Part 2

Historical Mediums and Forms of Mediumship

3

The Many Ways in Which Mediumship Can Show Itself

Mediumship is not new. Some form of spirit communication has been around since time immemorial. Ultimately, mediumship has its roots in shamanism, which is generally accepted dating back as far as the hunter-gatherer period. While practices may vary from culture to culture, this desire to know the unseen world tells us that spirit communication has always been an important—some might say essential—part of being human. Within our historical records, we see examples of spirit communication. Whether it is getting messages from the gods at the Oracle of Delphi or communing with spirits in the sitting room of a Victorian séance, human beings have sought a bridge to the higher side of life. Mediums are this bridge. By allowing themselves to be of service to the whole of society, they learn to master the ability to transcend their individuality and cultivate a sense of service for the benefit of those who utilize them, sometimes at a cost to themselves. The role of these individuals is valuable and important and remains so to this day.

As we explore the work of these specific mediums, we will also discuss the types of mediumship they took part in: mental mediumship, physical mediumship, trance mediumship, and healing. While this book is primarily focused on mental mediumship, we cannot fully explore mediumship without touching on these other forms. Learning about the different forms of mediumship will provide you with a well-rounded understanding of mediumship and its possible expressions. The more you understand the craft of mediumship, the better you will be.

Mental Mediumship

Mental mediumship is the form of mediumship where a medium relays messages from those in the spirit world to the recipient of the reading, the sitter. Mental mediumship is considered an active/passive form of mediumship. By this we mean the mind is active enough to engage the sitter while also being passive enough to receive information from the spirit communicator. To develop this, a medium learns to become sensitive by attuning their awareness to the energy within and around them. Then, once they are sensitive, they wait for the presence of the power to move them into a link with a spirit communicator. A link is the connection between the medium and the spirit. Through this link, the spirit communicator will pass impressions to the medium via the four clairs. The medium should be able to provide information that can be validated by the sitter. Once the sitter is satisfied that they can recognize who the spirit communicator is through the evidence provided, the medium may then relay a message from the spirit to the sitter.

Mental mediumship is the most common form of mediumship and what most people are familiar with. When you think of going to see a medium, this is the kind of reading most think of. Mental mediumship, like all forms of mediumship, is developed through dedicated sitting in the power and years of development in a spirit circle where practice sittings are done.

Physical Mediumship

Physical mediumship is the form of mediumship where various kinds of physical phenomena occur that are experienced by all present—mediumistic or not. Traditionally, the development of this form of mediumship required the use of a physical medium, someone who contains, within their biology and energy, the correct makeup to produce large amounts of a substance called ectoplasm. Ectoplasm is an energetic yet physical substance that is drawn from the orifices of a physical medium to produce some forms of physical phenomena. It can take the form of a gas, appearing as smoke or a mist; a malleable cloth-like substance; or a solid, such as long rods. Through physical mediumship, spirit phenomena as simple as cold breezes, spirit lights, and rapping and tapping in the séance room are common. As this form develops, more miraculous forms of phenomena can occur such as spirit trumpets (a cone-shaped object made out of metal or cardboard used to amplify disembodied spirit voices) or other objects being moved around a room by spirit, spirit voices speaking into the room (independent direct voice phenomena), and partial or full materialization of spirit presences in the room. Other forms of physical phenomena include levitation of objects such as tables or other objects, even a baby grand piano.

Ectoplasm is said to be sensitive to light; therefore, most demonstrations of physical mediumship, or séances, are held in minimal to no light. Ectoplasm is said to be dangerous to produce due to its physical connection to the medium. Because this physical substance is an extension of the medium, it has been claimed that mediums have been hurt upon a sudden burst of light or loud, unexpected sounds that caused the ectoplasm to snap back too quickly, resulting in burns and wounds.

However, some physical phenomena have been produced more recently without the use of ectoplasm. In the 1990s, a group known as the Scole Group, in Scole, England, produced incredible phenomena that were studied by the Society for Psychical Research and found to be genuine.[4] The spirit team working with the group used an energy-based alternative source that they termed *photoplasm*, which was not as light sensitive and did not exude from a specific medium but rather from the group's collective energy. Through this newer physical energy, unique phenomena were produced such as intricate and complex images appearing on unopened camera film, table levitation, healing spirit lights, and partial materializations of otherworldly beings. This phenomena is

---

4   G. Solomon and J. Solomon, *The Scole Experiment* (Waltham Abbey, Essex: Campion Books, 2006).

documented in the documentary *The Scole Experiment,*[5] which can be found online for free.

To develop this form of mediumship, traditionally someone must show physical mediumship potential, as it is believed that only certain individuals have the makeup necessary to produce this rare form of mediumship. However, one can begin to see if it can be developed by creating a home circle wherein a group of dedicated sitters meet each week religiously. Often, they are requested to sit in the same seats in the circle each week, and some even go so far as requiring the same clothes. The sittings are held in either red light or complete darkness because it is believed that the slower wavelength of red light has less of an impact on the ectoplasm, should it be produced. In these meetings, a medium is generally selected to sit in a small area enclosed by a sheet, known as a spirit cabinet. Here the physical medium sits and moves into a trance state. For physical mediumship to occur, generally, a medium needs to develop deep trance. Then the spirit world is able to use the energy created by the group to create the phenomena. However, the development of this kind of phenomena can take years to develop. Many groups give up sitting before any major phenomena occurs, hence the lack of physical mediums today.

Trance Mediumship

Trance mediumship is a form of mediumship that requires the awareness of the medium to become so passive that the spirit communicator is able to speak directly through the medium in their own words and stream of consciousness. Trance mediumship is considered a passive/passive form of mediumship because the mind of the medium is so disengaged as well as allowing a passive blending with the spirit communicator. Trance mediumship can take many forms.

---

5   YouTube, "The Afterlife Investigations," https://youtu.be/Mr6hOo8qLfM (accessed January 17, 2022).

Trance Philosophy

Trance philosophy is the most common form of trance that we see today. In general, trance philosophy is produced when a medium brings forward their spirit guide to speak on a given subject matter. Often, the information is pertinent to the life of those who listen, or they can also give great teachings and lessons for the benefit of all.

Trance Clairvoyance

Trance clairvoyance is a form of trance where the medium's spirit guide speaks directly through the medium and acts as the intermediary between the spirit communicator and the sitter. The medium has very little to do with the process; the medium's guide leads the communication. In theory, this should provide an even greater accuracy in the reading because the guide has more control over the medium and has a greater connection to the world of spirit, and therefore should be able to bring a clearer message.

Trance Communication

Trance communication is a form of trance mediumship where the medium goes into a trance and the spirit communicator can speak directly to the sitter using the medium's voice. In today's mediumship, we do not see this form often developed. However, in the past, this was one of the most common forms of mediumship readings. People would come to see a medium and get the chance to have a fully fluent conversation with their loved one in spirit. Excellent trance communicators could even speak fluently in languages that they did not speak normally.

Trance Art

Trance art is any form of mediumship where the medium enters into a trance state and art is produced. This can be painting, sculpting, music, and more. Generally, a trance artist will have a team of spirit artist helpers in the spirit world that wish to support the medium and bring through incredible works of art, often in unimaginably short periods of time.

Automatic Writing

Automatic writing is a form of trance mediumship where the spirit communicator is able to take full control of the hand of the medium and write out their own stream of consciousness. We often hear of people saying that they do automatic writing, but what they often mean is inspired writing, which is where you allow a stream of inspired words to come to your mind and you write them out. True automatic writing is much rarer and far more evidential. In genuine automatic writing, the medium might have their hand entranced while they are able to do some kind of complex task such as math with the other hand and mind. While this occurs, a perfectly separate stream of consciousness is being written out by the entranced hand. Moreover, a phenomenon called cross correspondences—where multiple entranced mediums share the same information all over the world—shows us that automatic writing can provide evidence of survival.

Healing Mediumship

Believe it or not, healing is considered a form of mediumship because it is the act of passing energy from a divine source to the receiver of the energy. Healing is considered a very special form of mediumship because of its ability to heal physical, mental, and emotional wounds. While there are many modalities to heal, energetic and trance healing are the two that will be discussed here. Neither form of healing is better or more effective than the other. Both are meant to facilitate healing in the recipient.

Energy Healing

Energy healing comes through a medium's ability to channel personal or universal energy. Energetic healers learn how to channel healing power and pass this over the recipient's body or wherever it is needed. While there are many forms of energy healing one can learn, ultimately the process is the same. The medium allows themselves to become a passive channel for spiritual energy to pass through them.

Trance Healing

Trance healing is a form of healing through the use of a healing spirit guide. These guides will entrance the medium and provide the healing directly to the recipient. They may speak to the recipient or merely pass the energy healing along. Trance healing differs from energetic healing in that a healing spirit guide uses the medium's body to bring through the healing energies. What makes trance healing interesting is that it accomplishes two things: one, it demonstrates survival of physical death, and two, it creates healing for those here in the physical world. This form of healing is unique in that it accomplishes both tasks in the same moment.

By exploring the many ways in which mediumship can show itself, we begin to realize that mental mediumship is just the tip of the iceberg when it comes to the amazing works that can be done through the power of the spirit. We should never limit the potential of what the spirit can do when we move out of the way and allow the spirit to use us however they can. I share these examples of incredible mediums of the past to begin planting seeds in your own awareness of how things that may seem impossible are possible and have already occurred. Trust in yourself; these people were no different than you or me. With time, dedication, and the right foundations under your belt, you too could develop incredible gifts of the spirit that are just as amazing if not more than those mentioned here.

Exceptional Mediums
of the Past

Knowing that mediumship has a meaningful place in society and our history, I felt it important to include a section on notable mediums in the history of Western mediumship—more specifically, those who have shaped and formed modern Spiritualism. I chose these specific examples because I believe honoring those who have made a notable impact on the current state of mediumship is important. They often labored to gain respect for the craft in the nineteenth and twentieth centuries. Also, I feel that the quality of work of the mediums I mention is exceptional. By having examples of what great mediumship can look like, we realize that extraordinary communication with the spirit world is possible and offers a place to rest the bar of quality mediumship upon. Finally, by understanding what has been possible with mediumship, perhaps we can discover where it is going and how we can build and expand upon the work that has come before us.

Examples of Mental Mediums

While there are many outstanding mental mediums of the past, I have selected two of my favorites due to their mental ability and their humility and heart for service. I highly recommend learning more about both these incredible mental mediums (see recommended resources).

Helen Hughes

Helen Hughes, also known as Helen the Beloved, was an English medium who worked in the early half of the twentieth century. She was known as a clairaudient, meaning she heard the spirit communicators just as clearly as normal voices. She explained she experienced the voices as coming from around her or within her solar plexus. Due to her incredible clairaudient ability, Mrs. Hughes gave some of the most remarkable evidence that we have ever had. Her level of specificity is rarely matched. Below is an example of a reading she gave that demonstrates her specificity.

> HELEN: There is a Mrs. Richardson in the gallery. I get the name Jimmie Richardson … He has brought William Clark with him … and Jimmie often saved him from trouble … Jimmie Richardson brings Robert and Lizzie, and also Mary Bewick. He tells me your godmother was Mary McIntyre, and she was in some way connected with an off-license for the sale of beer when you were fourteen to seventeen years of age.
>
> SITTER: Quite right![6]

I always like to share the mediumship of Helen Hughes because she is easily one of the greatest examples of what is possible when working with the spirit from an open-hearted and fully trusting place. While many will not necessarily reach this level of specificity due to the exceptional nature of her clairaudience, it does illustrate for us what is possible when we develop our mediumship. I am a firm believer that the same power that passed through Mrs. Hughes is the same power that passes through you. Therefore, if given enough work, you too can bring through incredibly accurate and specific information from those in spirit.

6   B. Upton, *The Mediumship of Helen Hughes* (London: The Psychic Book Club, 1946), 62, 63.

Albert Best

Albert Best is another example of incredible mediumship. He was a close friend of my mentor Gordon Smith, so I was fortunate enough to hear personal stories of Mr. Best's incredible abilities. After losing his wife and children in a bombing raid during World War II, Mr. Best became a postman. His mediumship was a service he provided to others due to his personal understanding of grief and loss. From this loss came great healing for many. Mr. Best was known for his accuracy in his readings, often providing full names and addresses. Due to his work as a postman and his familiarity with seeing names and addresses, Mr. Best would be shown an envelope in his mind's eye with the name and address of those in spirit wishing to communicate.

He was also known to be an incredibly humble and generous man who truly cared for the well-being of others. Gordon once shared with us a beautiful piece of wisdom from Mr. Best: "The deeper you've been hurt in this world, the deeper you can heal." While Mr. Best was by all accounts an exceptional medium, he is an excellent example of how the spirit world can provide you with incredible detail through the power of clairvoyance.

Examples of Physical Mediums

While physical mediumship has had its fair share of frauds and tricksters, I do not believe that all claims of physical mediumship can be lumped together. Below are two examples of excellent physical mediumship that I consider to be genuine and impressive.

Jack Webber

Jack Webber is considered one of the most photographed physical mediums. While never scientifically tested, Mr. Webber produced incredible examples of physical mediumship without the use of a cabinet and in darkened conditions. Through the use of infrared photography, many photos exist of his physical phenomena, including ectoplasmic rods. Mr.

Webber's mediumship is said to have produced many kinds of levitations, dematerializations, and spirit voices, both through the spirit trumpet and also independently speaking within the room. He was also an excellent healer. Mr. Webber's mediumship is an excellent example of the limitless physical bounds that the spirit world can provide for us when we truly hand over the control to the spirit world.

Alec Harris

Alec Harris is probably one of the most prolific physical mediums we have had. Harris was a materialization medium, meaning that his spirit helpers were able to draw from Harris a large amount of ectoplasm and create their physical forms out of this material. It was reported that he could have dozens of spirit people materializing in a given séance, often on the heels of the previous materialization. These materializations would come walking out of the cabinet with the entranced medium still in plain view. They would vary in shapes, sizes, ethnicities, and even gender. One notable materialization would appear as a busty woman, which was quite different to Harris's form. Not only that, there are many reports of watching these materializations build up and disperse in plain view of the sitters. The most beautiful thing about his mediumship was the evidential quality. These materializations were not just guides but loved ones of those in attendance. People were reunited, embraced by, and spoke with their loved ones. Alec Harris's mediumship is hailed as one of the finest materialization mediums there has ever been.

Leslie Flint

Leslie Flint is one of the most tested direct voice mediums we have had. Flint's séances were held in the dark, where voices would be heard as if coming from midair. The voices were of guides and loved ones for those in the séance. Interestingly, Flint hated going into trance, so his guides did not put him under their influence while the voices occurred. He could sometimes be heard having conversations with the voices while they were speaking. He was greatly tested by scientists, including being asked to hold a specific measurement of a colored liquid in his mouth, which was then duct-taped and plastered over at the start of a séance; at the end, he was asked to spit it out so they could measure that it was the same amount of liquid. Even under these conditions, the voices still came and spoke, ruling out ventriloquism. These séances and the voices were recorded and can be heard by visiting the Leslie Flint website (see recommended resources).

Examples of Trance Mediums

Trance mediumship was more common in the early part of the Spiritualist movement. It was common to expect that if you were to go see a medium, they would slip into a trance state and your loved one might communicate through them. Through these excellent examples of trance mediumship, beautiful art, philosophy, and evidential healing messages were conveyed.

Maurice Barbanell

Maurice Barbanell was the editor of the *Psychic News* and *Two Worlds*, two magazines that reported on Spiritualism, for over three decades. Interestingly enough, Mr. Barbanell developed trance mediumship and became the medium to the spirit guide Silver Birch. Through Mr. Barbanell, Silver Birch brought through some of the most treasured philosophy on life and spirituality to the Spiritualist movement. I always suggest students of mediumship explore the many recorded words and books of Silver Birch's teachings.

Gladys Osborne Leonard

An excellent example of a trance clairvoyant medium is Gladys Osborne Leonard. Hailed as the "Queen of Spiritualism" for the quality of her mediumship, she was extensively studied by the Society for Psychical Research. Mrs. Leonard discovered her trance abilities through table tipping. This is a form of spirit communication where the spirit world tips the table and taps out the corresponding numbers to letters of the alphabet. Through this, a message can be conveyed. After twenty-six unsuccessful sittings, her guide Feda communicated through the table. Shortly thereafter, she began to go into a trance state and Feda began speaking through her.

Mrs. Leonard and Feda were studied extensively. Feda would pass messages to the sitters regarding their loved ones' lives, often providing such specificity that many of the scientists who studied Mrs. Leonard were convinced of her authenticity. Not only that, Feda would often suggest to the researchers that she perform what is known as a "book test." In a book test, the entranced medium will describe in detail a room in the home of one of the scientists or sitters present. She would then tell them to look at a specific bookshelf in the room and give them descriptors to find a very specific book on a specific shelf with a certain number of books from the left or right. She would describe the binding of the book and then give a page number for them to turn to. She would describe what would be found on the page—either specific passages or the meaning on the page given.

Helen Hughes

Not only was Helen Hughes an incredible mental medium, she was also an outstanding trance medium. Mrs. Hughes was known to provide exceptionally evidential trance communication sittings where she would bring through loved ones in spirit to speak directly to the sitter. So incredible was her ability that she could speak fluently in languages not normally known to her. She has been reported to have spoken in Hindi, Swedish, Portuguese, and more.

Below is an excerpt where Hughes recounts an exceptional example of a message she gave while in trance, wherein she "spoke in tongues" unknown to her:

> The sender was a young Portuguese who had passed over not
> very long before. He happened to leave this world while he
> was in his sick bed listening-in to a broadcast commentary of
> a fight in which one of the boxers was Tommy Farr...he told

his mother, through me, of course—in perfect Portuguese—that he was keenly looking forward to witnessing the Farr-Louis world-title fight… My only language is my mother tongue.[7]

This is an exceptional example of quality trance mediumship. Mrs. Hughes shows us yet again how clearly the spirit world can use us when we allow ourselves to surrender completely to the influence of the other world.

José Medrado

An excellent example of a spirit artist is the Brazilian trance painter José Medrado. At one point in his development as a physical medium, he gave it up and was later approached by the spirit of Renoir, the French painter. When Renoir came to Medrado in 1988, he proposed "turning paint into bread"[8] to support an orphanage and community center called Ciadad da Luz, or "City of Lights." Since that time, Medrado has traveled around the world demonstrating his mediumship to groups of people, creating incredible works of art in minutes while in the trance state with the help of Renoir and other famous artists. He then auctions off the paintings to support the orphanage.

I have personally had the pleasure to watch Medrado work on three occasions, and it is quite incredible to watch, as well as to experience the smell that emanates from his energy when his spirit helpers draw near. It is a smell of ether and usually occurs when his spirit helpers bring healing energy. It is also reported that on one occasion, a butterfly he had painted materialized in the middle of the demonstration and flew around the room. People have also suggested that his paintings contain healing properties.

---

7   B. Upton, *The Mediumship of Helen Hughes* (London: The Psychic Book Club, 1946), 93.

8   Mediunidade José Medrado, Cidade da Luz, https://www.cidadedaluz.com.br/en/jose-medrado/mediumship/index.html (accessed January 18, 2022).

Leonora Piper

Leonora Piper is an incredible example of trance and automatic writing. Mrs. Piper was a housewife and trance medium from Boston, Massachusetts, in the early 1900s. She was studied by William James, a pioneering Harvard psychologist and a founder of the American Society for Psychical Research. Originally a skeptic, James became convinced of Mrs. Piper's authenticity after studying her for years in many scientifically controlled sittings. I mention her as an outstanding medium because of her ability to bring through multiple spirit communicators at once in trance. Mrs. Piper could go into a deep trance and bring forward one spirit communicator through her speaking, an entirely separate communicator through one hand, and yet another from her other hand, all at once.

Unfortunately for Mrs. Piper, she was subject to extreme treatment by the different scientists who studied her over the span of her career. She was poked, prodded, and even burned to test if she was truly in trance. While at times her mediumship could be inconsistent (like all mediumship), she is regarded as an excellent example of quality mediumship.

Examples of Healing Mediums

Likely some of the most documented Western energy healers of the twentieth century, the two mediums discussed below were contemporaries who demonstrated two ways to heal: energy healing and trance healing. Neither was better than the other, and both brought about extensive evidence of what was possible with spiritual healing.

George Chapman

One of my all-time favorite mediums is George Chapman and his spirit helper, Dr. Lang. Chapman became acquainted with his guide through the use of a makeshift talking board while he was working as a fireman. This communication eventually led to an entranced state where Dr.

Lang, Chapman's spirit guide, began speaking through him and providing healing to others. Chapman's trance was very clear and deep, which allowed Dr. Lang to work through him for hours a day. Even more interesting, Chapman's mediumship was so good that it convinced Dr. Lang's living daughter that her father was truly speaking through the entranced Chapman. She was so convinced that it was her father that she struck a deal with Chapman to have regular sittings with her and former colleagues of Lang's.

What's more, Lang's healings through Chapman are highly documented throughout the many years of his career. While Lang never promised cures, he always said he would do his best, and cures were often the result of his work.

Harry Edwards

Harry Edwards was an English medium in the twentieth century and was exceptional at his work. He would regularly hold demonstrations of his healing ability where dramatic and often unbelievable accounts of healings were reported. He especially would select people with very obvious ailments, like a goiter or growth, and then create vast improvements right before the eyes of everyone present. He would even invite doctors to follow the patients and confirm the healing had occurred. This brought him great notoriety for his healing abilities. He was a healer of the highest order, and his methods are still taught to this day.

There is not enough room in this chapter (or this book) to cover all of the incredible mediums Spiritualism has developed throughout history. Moreover, there are surely countless others who do not fall under the umbrella of Spiritualism and yet have provided incredible evidence of survival and spirit communication. I believe it is so important for us to learn about mediums of the past, if for no other reason than to show what spirit is capable of. Those mentioned in this chapter were normal, ordinary folks who put their trust in the spirit world and allowed themselves to be guided and led to do incredible things. If they can do it, so can you.

If you found any of the aforementioned mediums interesting, see the recommended resources for more details.

Part 3

Before You Begin

Ethics of Mediumship
and Psychic Work

One of the most important things I try to impress upon my students is the importance of ethical mediumship. Ethical mediumship is abiding by a practical and grounded code of conduct that ensures a high standard of mediumship and protection for the sitter. It is so important for anyone wanting to develop their mediumship to work with the highest moral standards because mediumship has many detractors that claim we are defrauding people and preying on the grieving. While we know we are doing true, genuine spirit communication, it would be wrong to say that all who claim to do this work are working to the highest standard of morality and with the best intentions for their clients. Unfortunately, for every genuine, ethical medium, there are a handful of frauds.

Since even before the Fox sisters claimed to have heard knocking on the walls of their cottage, mediumship has had to battle the issue of frauds, fakes, and con artists. In fact, a large part of the scientific inquiry into mediums has been around trying to catch them out as frauds—and many successfully did! Harry Houdini, the great magician, made it an important point in his life to prove that mediums were frauds. In fact, he and his wife had an agreed-upon message to send to one another through a medium if they were able to communicate from the spirit world. Interestingly enough, this coded message was delivered to Harry's wife years after his death in a series of séances with a medium named Arthur Ford, though there is controversy regarding its authenticity.

The decoded message was "Rosabelle, believe." Initially Houdini's wife believed the message was true and accurate. She signed a letter stating she fully believed, only later to recant this after theories on how Ford could have received the message were reported. One such report was that Ford gleaned the coding key from a book that was published about Houdini a year before. However, having read the part of the book that discusses this key, I personally do not think he could have gleaned the message from just understanding the code. While it remains unclear in this instance if there was fraud, it should be mentioned that many years later in his career, a message given by Ford on national television was found to be information he knew beforehand, acquired by normal means. This puts his previous messages in question.

There are many examples throughout the whole of mediumship and spiritualism in general that are much like the above story. "Mixed mediumship" is a term used to describe genuine mediums who at times produce real phenomena and at other times are purely fraudulent. This is the challenge we face as mediums wanting to do quality and genuine work. Where there is fame or money to be made, there are often frauds and fakes. These tend to be the greatest motivators for fraud. The challenging part is what to believe when we know that there are those who would wish to fool us and those who do genuine work with the spirit. Those who are eager to believe will not question the authenticity of an experience, and those who cannot believe will always find a mundane explanation, but this provides an even greater need for a neutral, grounded, and critical approach to mediumship in all its forms. While there will always be those looking to fool others, there are still those who do genuine and honest mediumship.

I have had the unfortunate, albeit valuable lesson of knowing fraudulent mediums personally. This has been one of the greatest disappointments of my career—to know that there are those who would fool or take advantage of grieving people. However, I have also had the privilege to have worked with mediums who exemplify the height of integrity and ethical mediumship. This is why I am so passionate about integrity in all things related to your spiritual work and development. As the researcher William James wrote about Mrs. Piper, "If you wish to upset the law that all crows are black, you must not seek to show that no crows are; it is enough if you prove one single crow to be white."[9] I hope that you will be a white crow amongst the many black. The more that we can hold the standard of mediumship high, the more we can show the reality of spirit communication and what genuine mediumship looks like.

What does it mean to be a medium with integrity? Integrity means that you hold yourself to a high moral standard. In mediumship, this means being honest about what you can and cannot do. Yes, fraudulence is a dramatic form of being unethical, but more often unethical behavior comes in much more subtle ways. The medium may not even be aware that certain behaviors are considered unethical. With this in mind, let's explore important ethical behaviors and standards that will help you to maintain integrity in your work as a medium.

Boundaries

The importance of the development of boundaries within your mediumship cannot be overemphasized. To have boundaries is to have the awareness of when it is appropriate to link in with the spirit world or receive psychic information. It is the combination of self-discipline, self-awareness, and social awareness. It is self-discipline in that a developing medium needs to have control of their spiritual awareness and know how to regulate it. This means turning your mediumship on when it is time to use it and turning it off when it is not. This can sometimes feel unclear for some when they begin their journey. We want to only be connected to the spirit world when we are in an appropriate time and space, such as our meditative practice, our development circle, or when

---

9   R. Somerlott, *The Medium Had the Message*, https://www.americanheritage .com/medium-had-message (accessed January 24, 2022).

we have been asked to give a message or been given permission by the recipient of a message to provide one for them. We do not want to be open at other times. This is very important in cultivating discernment between what is your mind and what is coming from the spirit world. If we are open all the time, we will start blurring the lines between these two states of awareness. Also, it is a waste of your energy. Generally, if someone wants to be open all the time, there is something that they are trying to prove or show to those who are around them. Realize that you are meant to be in the normal world and that the times we connect with the spirit is when we are asked to or for our own personal development.

It is also important to remember that just because you become aware of psychic or mediumistic information, you do not need to pass it on. It is unethical to provide a reading or enter someone's energy without their consent. Would you like it if someone went into your purse without asking? No. It is the same with our energy. We need to respect others' space and not try to pick up energetic information, whether psychic or mediumship, without the express consent of the recipient. If you find that you can't help but give a message, recognize this is your ego wanting validation clothed in service to the spirit.

While it is important for mediums to have boundaries in their own mediumship, it is also important for the medium to set boundaries for their sitters. The lack of boundaries with your client often shows itself by your client becoming dependent on readings from you. It is important for you to learn to recognize when a client is seeing you too much and overly relying on spiritual answers rather than their own. Be sure to encourage your client to make decisions for themselves; it is their life, after all, and they have to live it. A mediumship reading should be a rare occurrence, especially if your client wants to connect with the same spirit communicator. Psychic readings should also be done no more than every three months at the most frequent, especially if they are on the same topic. Even longer intervals are preferred. We want our clients to live their own lives and be empowered to do so on their own.

To this end, it is important that the medium does not force their opinion or ideas on their client as a "must do." The spirit world never demands or dictates what should be done. They can make suggestions, but it is up to the individual to decide what action to take. The spirit world is never angry or disappointed in us if we do not do what they say, and neither should the medium be. Mediums must learn to offer what they can and then let go of the reading. This is having boundaries between yourself and your work. We want to do our best, then forget the rest.

Understand Your Limits

While a medium can do a lot in the way of helping others, it is important to know when you have reached your limit in your helpfulness. By this I mean a medium will not have all the answers all the time. We cannot expect ourselves to be the solution or have the answers to everyone's problems. Moreover, we as mediums are merely messengers providing information from the spirit realm to the sitter. Unless you have other training that allows you to support your client in other ways, such as a therapist license or medical training, you should not offer advice that is outside of your scope of education.

Yes, a medium can be inspired with information beyond their normal awareness; however, it is unethical to provide this information without the proper credentials. There are times where a client may come to you and what they do not need is a psychic or mediumship reading, but rather professional help in some other form. Take the time to reflect on what you can help with and offer. For anything beyond that, a referral is always appropriate.

Fear-Based Readings

While discussed briefly before, it bears repeating that the spirit world will not bring forward any kind of information that creates unnecessary fear or anxiety. If the spirit world brings forward any messages that may seem challenging, it will always come with the solution or how to mitigate whatever is arising. Mediums should not be quick to offer this kind of information to their sitters because it is almost always stemming from the medium's mind rather than the spirit world. It is also important to know that how you deliver the information can make a huge difference in how it is received. Just by adjusting the delivery of the information you receive, you can change it from something that could create fear or anxiety and present it in such a way that it feels reassuring and hopeful.

Unethical Information: Predicting Death, Disease, Divorce, or Disaster

Along the lines of fearful information, we should understand our limitations in the usefulness or helpfulness of certain types of information. Particularly as it relates to mediumship, there is no instance where the spirit world would discuss the four D's—death, disease, divorce, or disaster. While the spirit world can talk about the past experiences of these topics, any kind of prediction in any of these areas is likely to only create anxiety and fear in the sitter. It is highly unlikely the spirit would bring this kind of information to a mediumship reading in the future tense.

We should also be mindful never to diagnose any kind of physical health condition as a medium. Even if I were to sense something going on with a sitter, I would not say that they have whatever I am sensing. In the rare instance that I felt very compelled to mention something in the body, I may ask if they have noticed anything in a specific area. If they answered yes, I may suggest that they check in with their physician. However, I would not create any alarm or fear around it. In my years of reading, this scenario has occurred fewer times than I can count on one hand.

Ethics of Development

Just as it would be unethical for a first-year med student to be out working with the public, so too is it unethical for an underdeveloped medium to be working with the public. Especially with mediumship, we are dealing with grieving people in a very vulnerable state. We need to be very solid and confident in our mediumship before offering readings to anyone in this state. For most, this takes years of development and practice. Being self-aware in knowing where you are in your development is vital to protecting sitters from potential harm, as well as ensuring you are presenting yourself in the best possible way. There is no need to rush your development; there will always be a need for your service to others in this way. Take your time, and when you are truly well developed, you will be a great asset to many.

6

Understand Potential Sources of Tension So You Can Surrender

As you begin your mediumship journey, know that it will be a path of highs and lows, challenges and victories, tears of joy and tears of frustration. This is normal and a healthy part of self-discovery. If it was simple, we would all be doing it. Therefore, I invite you to be willing to fail, succeed, and trust yourself. Mediumship is all about learning to surrender to whatever is happening in the moment. This will be an ongoing theme throughout your journey, and it is the reason that mediumship takes so much time to develop. Not because the spirit is not ready and willing, but rather because we are learning to let go of control and develop our ability to relax and surrender.

Mediumship works best when we are free from tension and trying. Tension is the feeling we experience when we are trying to create a specific outcome, looking for or attempting to experience something from the spirit communicator, or reaching for more information. Tension is anything that causes us to feel like we are trying. Tension causes our energy to contract and moves our awareness into our thinking mind. When we move into our thinking mind, we are no longer centered in a feeling, sensing space, and we are not attuned to our energetic senses. Therefore, it is important for us to learn the causes of tension and how we can move past them and maintain our connection to our spiritual awareness.

To this end, we need to understand what causes tension in our mediumship. In my journey of learning all I could about mediumship, I was fortunate enough to come across an incredible medium named Eileen Garrett. Mrs. Garrett had a great interest in understanding her mediumship. On the topic of accessing her spiritual abilities, she said,

> I am often asked what is the state of mind in which one is most able to function as a sensitive. I believe that the beginnings of this state lie in the development of an inner calm which is free from distraction or desire. The slightest effort to consciously produce evidence will inhibit this condition…In mediumship the goal is not only to be at one with oneself, but with all else in the universe.[10]

Here Garrett teaches us that even the slightest bit of tension or effort inhibits one's mediumistic awareness. She also offers us two sources from which tension derives—desire and distraction. Through my years of teaching and personally exploring my mediumship, I have also added a third inhibiting source of tension: expectation. Through recognizing how desire, distraction, and expectation create tension in our mediumship, we can learn how to counter them and thereby free our mediumship.

Desire

If you imagine for a moment what the experience of desiring something feels like, you will be able to recognize the subtle tension that is created from it. Whenever we are experiencing desire, there is a sense of reaching out, extending toward, or wanting to actively bring something to us. This subtle tension is enough to inhibit the mediumistic states of awareness.

---

10   E. Garrett, "Ethics of Mediumship," *Tomorrow Magazine* 8, no. 4, https://fst .org/spiritual-teachings/the-ethics-of-mediumship (accessed January 23, 2022).

When working with our mediumship, desire expresses itself in the desire to get correct information, the desire to do well, the desire to please the sitter, the desire to get a specific kind of information, etc. Any kind of wanting for a specific outcome falls under the realm of desire. And to be fair, wanting to do well and get correct information makes a lot of sense. Of course we want to do well and bring forward the best information we can. However, when we decide we are going to begin to connect with the spirit world, this desire will actually lead us away from the outcomes we want. Therefore, it is important for us to learn to set aside this desire when it is time to connect with the spirit. To do this, we must learn to become indifferent to the outcome of our reading. It sounds hard, but through learning where this desire comes from, we can change our reaction.

All forms of desire tend to stem from the ego wanting validation of some sort. Whether that is the validation of getting correct information or to not look like a fraud or a fool, we are looking to protect our egos from embarrassment. Therefore, to change this orientation, we need to realize that whether we are successful in our reading or not, it does not matter. I can hear you thinking, "But Michael, isn't learning to get real and accurate information the whole point of this book?" Yes, of course it is, but you have to put that desire aside when you are connecting to the spirit. Instead, make your focus surrendering and letting go. Rather than focus on getting things right, the question each medium should ask themselves is, "How much can I relax and get out of the way? How much can I hand this experience over to the spirit?"

By turning our attention to surrendering and relaxing, we take the tension out of trying to accomplish the outcome of the reading. Instead, our focus helps us foster the mindset needed to get clear communication from the world of spirit. Simply put, a medium's job is to become energetically sensitive by opening their energy through surrender and relaxation. Then, in this sensitive state, they wait for the change in the atmosphere or within their awareness. Lastly, they describe their experience as it unfolds. If you can make your focus "I just need to describe what's changing in my experience moment to moment," you will do much better than trying to focus on getting specific information or getting it right. This is how we cultivate indifference to the outcome—just give what you get and forget the rest.

During my development with Gordon Smith, he shared a story from his experience working at the Spiritualist Association of Great Britain that I feel describes the nature of mediumship quite well. While working there, they would be tasked to give around ten short readings on a given day. He explained that during the course of these ten readings, the first, second, third, and fourth reading might be fantastic. On the fifth, he may have gotten nothing. The sixth may have been excellent. The seventh reading might go okay, and the eighth, ninth, and tenth excellent again. I feel that this example helps to highlight the nature of our mediumistic awareness: it is inconsistent.

Sure, as we develop our consistency improves, but I feel that it illustrates an important point as it relates to desire. Sometimes you will do incredibly well; other times it will be a struggle. All you can do is give what you are experiencing and leave it at that. There is no expectation that your readings are going to be perfect every time. This is a false pressure we put on ourselves. This may help you in relieving the pressure on yourself for the desire to get it right or be "perfect." Unfortunately for you, you are not a robot where I can put a quarter in you and you'll spit out a crossed-over loved one. You are a human being, and sometimes it won't work the way you want it to. That is okay. There will be other readings where you shine.

Distraction

A large portion of a medium's development is learning mind control, or how we gain control over the way our mind reacts to the thoughts and stimuli that come into it. This is a lifelong journey of practice and conditioning our focus and awareness. This is the first type of distraction we must learn to overcome: the distraction of your own thoughts. If you have ever tried meditating, you will have experienced the overactivity of the mind. *What am I having for lunch after this? I have to remember to call my mom back. Is that the refrigerator I hear buzzing in the background?* Our mind, when tasked to quiet or focus, often will begin to look for any stimulus it can because it wants to be working. It is our job to learn to quiet this mind through meditative focus. Learning how to notice thoughts without engaging them will teach our mind to stay focused on what we wish it to. Also, giving your thinking mind something to do—such as focusing on the breath or focusing on the sensations in your body—will help you begin to train your overly active mind. By overcoming this, we can allow our awareness to learn how to become passive and receptive and thereby connect with the spirit world more easily. While having an overly active mind is one form of distraction we must learn to overcome, it is not the only kind of distraction a medium will experience.

Distraction of your own biases is another stumbling block for the developing medium. Whenever we meet the sitter we are doing a reading for, we can sometimes allow our own thoughts and feelings about this person to affect our opinion or assessment of them. Someone's age, gender, sexual orientation, race, religion, and cultural background can trigger biases we may have and contaminate our readings.

For example, say you had a young woman of eighteen come to you for a sitting. You begin to become sensitive and feel into the atmosphere around you. You sense the presence of a mother and father in spirit; however, due to the woman's age, you doubt yourself because she seems too young to have a mother and father in spirit. This doubt is the mind entering into your reading and already distracting you from what is coming from the spirit. As it turns out, both her parents died suddenly and they were who she was hoping to connect to. We cannot assume any kind of information about our sitter. We have to learn to just give what we are experiencing.

Another example of biases entering into the reading comes from my own experiences as a sitter for other developing mediums. Due to my ethnically ambiguous appearance, people often cannot place where I am from. I have had the uncomfortable experience of being told "facts" about my life based on the perceived ethnic group another developing medium believed me to be. The person who was acting as my partner, for one particular exercise, believed I was from Mexico. They described a picture of my life that included ranch-style homes, chihuahuas, stone maize grinders, and tortillas. In an entirely different instance, another person giving me a reading told me about all the saris, bindis, and spices my family had because they thought I was Indian. Unfortunately for my partners, none of these were correct, but it does illustrate how the mind of the medium can enter into a reading based on the distractions of their own preconceived ideas about their sitter.

To counter this form of distraction, we need to trust ourselves and what we are experiencing from the other world. We cannot make any assumptions based on how someone presents. Just describe your experience as it is happening without adding anything to it. The worst that can happen is your sitter will say no. But also, we need to be mindful about what our own opinions and thoughts are of people who look or act differently than ourselves so that we can tell when our mind is coming into the reading. When I give a reading to someone, I come to it with the assumption that this person can be from anywhere, have any kind of lived experience, and that their appearance or behavior does not indicate the kind of life they have led. They could be adopted for all I know. Approach each reading with a clean slate and just describe your experience as it unfolds.

The last form of distraction is the most common: distraction by our sitter. As an example of what I mean by being distracted by your sitter, first imagine that a friendly, warm lady comes to you for a reading. She smiles at you as you greet her and laughs and jokes with you prior to your sitting. As you provide her with information, she is attentive, responsive, and effusive in her affirmative answers. This would likely cause you to feel relaxed, calm, and enjoy the message. In truth, it would likely create a very positive reading outcome. Now imagine a man comes to you for a reading: his arms are crossed, he has a grimace on his face, and as you give him information, he begrudgingly gives you a yes. While you are getting correct information, he comes across as reserved and cautious. Imagine how you would feel in this kind of reading. You can feel the tension that is building within you, can't you? It is an uncomfortable situation, and yet we would still need to do our best to not become distracted by the responses of our sitter. Whether our sitter is effusive and open or reserved and quiet, we should treat their reaction to what we are saying the same way—that is, with a sense of neutrality. If we allow ourselves to become too involved with our sitters' responses, we will constantly be drawn out of our connection to the spirit. Even if our sitter is more neutral but at points gives us a look of uncertainty or confusion over something we have just given, we need to not react to how they are presenting. This could cause us to start to search for information because we can tell by their face that they cannot understand what we are giving. This is when the mind will want to jump in and cause you to start straining due to the tension you are feeling.

To counter this form of distraction, we need to become less interested in the way our sitter responds and more connected to our spirit communicator. To achieve this, we need to employ the 90/10 rule of mediumship. This rule states that we should have 90 percent of our attention on the spirit communicator and only 10 percent of our attention on the sitter in front of us. By doing this, we are becoming much more connected and involved with our link to the spirit communicator and thereby staying connected to them regardless of how our sitter is responding. Also, the more your attention is on the experience you are having with spirit, the less inclined you are to pay excessive attention to your sitter. If you find that your attention is still too attached to the reaction of the sitter, you may be experiencing the desire to please your sitter, in which case I would suggest that you revisit the section on desire again.

Expectation

Remember the story of my discovery of my mediumistic ability at the beginning of the book? I shared how the very first reading I ever did was the ideal reading. I received names, dates, relationships, and more, but when I tried to connect the next week, I got nothing—and the following week after that and after that. I can now recognize that this was due to the tension source, expectation. Expectation is the idea that the way we experience something one time will be experienced that way again.

In the example from my journey, I had the experience of information just coming to me effortlessly. Why? Because I had no expectation of how it should look, feel, or be. I was able to be present in the experience and describe what was happening to me. This is exactly how mediumship works the best: when it is free of expectation. Therefore, as soon as I had an idea of what was possible, I then expected that it should happen the same exact way again. But having an experience to compare it to, I was no longer relaxed, indifferent, or free. I had placed pressure on myself built by the expectation that I would be good at bringing information forward as well as the pressure from the expectations of the other students that I was "good" at this. Expectation creates tension that does not allow us freedom in our mediumship; therefore, our energy closes down.

Expectation can also come from our preconceived ideas of how we *think* we should be experiencing something. This is often the case for new students just coming into mediumship because they have expectations on how they think it should work. Most students do not recognize how subtle the experience of mediumship is, so when they begin to connect with the spirit, they are missing the signs and information coming to them. They are expecting it to be obvious and clear, so their mind tunes out the actual spiritual information. This can also happen when a medium expects that they work in a specific way. For example, many students believe that they are clairvoyant first, and therefore ignore the sensing-feeling experience of their clairsentience. However, once they begin to work with other students in practice readings, they find that their images are incorrect, originating from the mind rather than from the spirit. I often have to get them to focus on their clairsentience, which almost always leads them to get correct information. This is because the spirit is using their clairsentience to bring information to them rather than their clairvoyance as they previously expected.

To counter expectation as a source of tension in our mediumship, we must learn to treat each reading as if it were the first time every time. Knowing what I know now after all these years of development, I would tell my younger self to let go of the previous reading completely. Treat each reading as you move forward as if you have never done a reading before. This mindset helps you to be present in the experience without looking for something specific or trying to go get information. I would have also told younger me to just describe exactly what is coming without out expectation of how that might look or feel. The more he could be neutral about the process, the better.

Tension within our mediumship is the biggest inhibitor of our sensitive states of awareness, whether mediumship or psychism. By learning to manage desire, distraction, and expectation, we free our mediumship from tension and pressure. The less pressure we have in our mediumship, the easier information flows to us from the spirit world. If you imagine your connection to the spirit as a tube through which information flows through, the more tension you have and the more the tube contracts. The more relaxed you are, the more the tube dilates. Tension will stop the flow of information that is coming to you. Stay neutral, relaxed, and indifferent to the outcome in order for your mediumship to best work.

7

Become Familiar with Grief

As a medium, the emotion you will experience the most from your sitters other than love and hope is grief. Grief is often the reason a sitter comes to you in the first place. Therefore, it is incredibly vital that you understand grief to the best of your ability. While I cannot cover the whole topic of grief in this one chapter, I can offer you some of what I have learned as a medium regularly working with grieving people. I will also share with you my perspective on grief and how the medium fits in with this.

To begin, it is important to recognize that mediums cannot take away grief for someone else; no one can. In fact, grief is a normal and healthy part of someone's journey in life. If you live long enough, you will experience grief at some point in your life. So if mediums cannot take away grief, what can they do?

The job of the medium is to open the minds and hearts of those who have lost loved ones to the possibility of life beyond death. When I say life beyond death, I don't necessarily mean the spiritual afterlife. More specifically, I am referring to the life of the sitter beyond the death of a loved one. If you have lost someone, you may recognize the feeling that the world has stopped when your loved one passed. So many feelings of confusion, helplessness, loss, and questions left unanswered often linger after they have crossed over. It can feel like someone has hung up the phone forever. It is here, at the moment of death, that so many find it hard to move beyond. When their loved one passed away, so did their own lives the way they knew it before. The grieving person can often stay in this place, replaying the loss and their sense of the life they knew before being gone. Mediums can play a role in supporting their process of healing. We can help show them that life continues on—not only for the spirit of their loved one, but by showing that if their loved one's life goes on, so can their own. The medium offers the gift of awareness that can open the door to the hope that one day they will be reunited again as well as the acknowledgment that their loved one is not truly gone—just different. It is our job as mediums to try to change people's understanding and relationship to death, for what we know is that death is just a transition—an event along the journey of life, not an ending to it.

Mediums offer a glimpse into what can be expected when we make that transition from this form into the next. It is our job to show that our loved ones in spirit continue to evolve, grow, and maintain an avid interest in our lives and that their lives continue on. Grieving people are desperately searching for something that proves this fact. In this way, they are hoping to find something that can relieve them from the sense of loss, which often feels like a thick cloud or storm over their lives. It is the job of the medium to offer hope to those who have lost it. We have to learn to be the rock in the storm of grief; by doing so, we offer a life vest to those who cannot remember what it's like to feel joy and peace in life. Through our work, we remind our sitters that there is something more past this grief.

To best support our sitters, it is important for us to be familiar with grief. Perhaps you have been touched by it firsthand or, like myself, you were fortunate enough to have experienced it for the first time well into your adulthood. In either case, let us explore common experiences of grief so we may be more mindful and present for where our grieving client may be at in their healing journey.

Remain Compassionate and Nonjudgmental

There is no right or wrong way to grieve. Some will jump into the business of taking care of the loose ends and clearing out the unfinished tasks that often occur upon a loved one's passing. Others will find themselves unable to get out of bed, crippled in the loss. Still others may feel a sense of relief mixed with their sense of loss. None of these are right or wrong. Avoid any kind of judgment on how someone "should" feel when someone close to them passes away. As a medium, you quickly learn that relationships are multifaceted and multilayered. Someone can grieve an abusive husband or feel relief after a family member passes by suicide. While these may seem counterintuitive, we do not know the whole story of someone's relationship or why these feelings may be true. We must therefore meet each sitter who comes to us with this same level of nonjudgment. We cannot truly be supportive of someone if we are in judgment of them. Whatever your feelings about a given situation, it is not a factor when working as a medium. We are a neutral party who bring presence, a safe space, and information that passes from us to the sitter. We are nothing more than a receiver passing information. How a relationship sounds to us as we deliver information has no bearing on the facts of the reading. We merely report the news; we don't comment on it.

This same level of compassion and openness must also extend to our sitter's emotional state. When in grief, people can behave in ways they normally would not. When you feel your whole world has ended, it can create a primal survival response. This can express itself in extreme mood swings or behaviors, such as laughter to tears very quickly or excessive spending or eating. We need to hold space for our sitters' emotional state with a sense of compassion.

More specifically, I am reminded of the kind of sitter who is desperate to have some kind of evidential proof that their loved one continues on. They likely have gone to many mediums and have left disappointed time after time, which is how they find themselves in front of you. These sitters can often come across as easily agitated or even aggressive for evidence or proof that their loved one is okay and well. They can be very challenging sitters, but we shouldn't turn them away or hold this against them. Perhaps they process their emotions differently than other sitters. This is not wrong or bad. While some sitters may come to you in a daze or haze brought on by the shock of their loss, sitters like this are keenly searching, and when they come up short, it creates frustration and further loss and disappointment. Have compassion for these sitters. In other circumstances, it is very possible that they would be much more open and available. Remember that they are suffering, and this is how it is playing out for them.

The Five Stages of Grief

To help us better understand the kinds of emotions that may arise, it is helpful to become familiar with Kübler-Ross's model called the five stages of grief.[11] Grief is unique to each person, and this model may not fit everyone's experience. However, it is helpful to have a starting point to work with as we become familiar with grief in our clients. The five stages of grief are denial, anger, bargaining, depression, and acceptance. It is important to understand that these stages are not linear in any way and can change rapidly or repeat themselves at any point in the journey. One can begin with anger and quickly move to acceptance, only to return to anger and then denial. There is no right order or arrival point with grief. However, understanding where someone is in this journey at a given moment is helpful.

---

11   E. Kübler-Ross and I. Byock, *On Death and Dying* (New York: Macmillan, 1969).

Denial

In this stage of grief, there is commonly a feeling of shock, overwhelm, and wondering how we can continue on. Reality has completely shifted in this stage of grief. Each day is a struggle to get through, and we can feel confused as to why this has happened or that it can't be real. The benefit of this stage is that it can help us handle our grief little by little, rather than the intensity of the reality all at once.

Anger

Anger is a common feeling in grief. It can be directed at people, events, or God. A commonly expressed feeling is "Why did God allow this to happen?" Anger is a helpful emotion because it is an action-oriented feeling. Where grief can often leave us feeling lost at sea, anger is something to hold on to and it is important to feel. It can often help those grieving to find structure in the world again. By processing anger and allowing the experience of it to be felt, the grieving individual can begin to reconnect to reality again.

Bargaining

Bargaining is often experienced as loss is occurring. Generally directed at a higher power, the grieving person can want to make a deal or a plea to not allow this loss to happen. Panic is often felt here. We can also look back on our interactions with who we have lost: "If only I had said this" or "If I had just done that." We may feel regret for the way things were left or words spoken. There is a sense of hopelessness that can come at the end of bargaining when we realize we do not have control over the outcome.

Depression

Depression generally comes when the grieving person is realizing the reality of their loss and feeling this loss more intensely. They can often feel alone and isolated. The sadness can grow into an overwhelming state. This is a natural part of grieving, but it is incredibly challenging.

It is important for those in this state to know there are people who still care. While it may not have much value for them in this state, it is there to call upon if they need to or are able to.

Acceptance

Acceptance does not mean that the grieving person is no longer feeling pain or loss; rather, they are no longer fighting the painful feelings, the reality of the loss, or trying to change the situation. There is acceptance to the reality of the loss even if other painful feelings still remain.

Having an awareness of this model for understanding grief is helpful, at the very least, to be able to hold a nonjudgmental space for those who come to you. Understanding that any one of the wide variety of emotions surrounding grief are at play helps us meet our sitters where they are and extend our compassion to them.

Allow Grief to Be Processed

As a medium, it is important to also recognize when we cannot help someone. Some people are not ready to receive a reading at that moment. There are instances where the grief is so palpable that the sitter can barely register what you are saying. They may have a sense of confusion or have a hard time remembering simple facts about their loved one. This would be an example of someone who requires some time to process their grief before seeking a medium. It would be appropriate for the medium to compassionately explain this and maybe in this instance just listen to their sitter. There have been times with sitters in this state that they actually benefited more from me listening to their concerns and sharing my knowledge about the spirit world rather than making a link, which began to help them shed some of the weight of grief. Later, they returned with a clearer mind and were able to receive the communication from their loved one.

With the process of grief, there is no timeline of what it should look or feel like. In fact, some never fully recover from the loss. Instead, they learn to live with it. Days do get easier and life can become livable again, but within them they carry the badge of loss on their heart for the rest of their lives. As mediums, we want to recognize that just because we can prove survival, we cannot take away someone's grief. We can support them and offer an opportunity to have a greater understanding of life and death, we can offer hope of reunion, we can offer evidence of survival, but we cannot take away their grief. This is their journey and theirs alone. We cannot be attached to the outcome of the reading and whether it has helped them or not. We can only be a support along the way and deliver what we are aware of.

The job of the medium is to be the rock in the storm of grief. We must learn how to manage and maintain a sense of compassionate neutrality with our sitter. It does not benefit our sitter in any way if we join them in their grief. This is a common mistake made by mediums who are not developed in understanding grief. Instead of moving the sitter through the experience of emotions, they stop and unintentionally point out the feelings being felt by the sitter by asking things like "Are you okay? Do we need to stop?" rather than continuing on with the reading. Others may join their sitter in their grief by overly sympathizing with what they are going through, becoming tearful or even full-on crying. It does no good to join your sitter in their grief. It is hard enough on their own. Instead, a medium should continue the reading and move through the emotional ups and downs unfazed by what occurs. The emotional ups and downs of your sitter are healthy, natural, and important for them to feel. Do not fear them or allow them to make you feel uncomfortable. Continue to pass the information as it happens. By allowing the sitter to experience their emotions as they occur in a nonjudgmental environment, we are creating a safe space for the spirit to do its work. After all, healing is the heart of mediumship, and this is the kind of healing that mediums do.

Mediums Experience Grief, Too

I also feel it is important to recognize that mediums are not exempt from grief. Grief is a social, human response to loss. While it is easy to say, "Oh, but you know they are okay and that they go on; surely you shouldn't grieve," it denies the fact that mediums are human beings. We want to be able to hug and hold our loved ones just as much as anyone else. The sense of loss is just as deep and as painful for us as it would be for anyone else. What we do benefit from is the knowing that we will see our loved one again, and oftentimes we are able to eventually experience our loved one coming near.

I know for myself, after my first personal, great loss of a loved one, I could not feel anything from the spirit world in the first month after their transition. My grief was so thick and deep that I had no awareness of the spirit world. It was a hard time, but it did cultivate in me the compassion and understanding as to what those who come to me live with and experience. What I knew about life after death meant very little in that state. While I knew spirit continued on for others, I was desperate for a sign or a message that might prove to me that *my* loved one continued on. I knew proof was possible, but I had not received the experience for myself. It was not until two months later that I finally received a personal connection with my loved one. It was powerful and special and, unsurprisingly, came out of nowhere when I was least expecting it.

Grief Can Make It Difficult to Connect

This is the challenge that most people have in connecting with their loved ones after they have passed. They have so much desire and tension in wanting to connect that they are not made available to the spirit world to receive. It is no fault of their own, but it is often the reason that a connection cannot be made. Sitters will often say to me, "Michael, why hasn't my loved one made a connection with me yet? I try and try and try and I never hear a thing. Help me to connect, please!" It is not that the spirit of their loved one isn't present or able to make a connection, but rather that we have to be in the receptive state to experience something from our loved ones. As we will discuss further, the passive, neutral, and receptive state is required to make a link.

That being said, I do want to encourage anyone who is struggling to make a link to let go of trying to make a connection and instead focus on a feeling of love for your loved one in spirit. Play their favorite song; let yourself cry, laugh, and remember the good times. These are the things that will help move you closer to being able to experience them not just in memory but in spirit form as well. Let go of any expectations that their message or visitation needs to look, feel, or be any specific way. Also recognize that the divine timing of when a spirit visitation or communication happens is far more powerful and meaningful than when we may want or demand it. Yes, we may feel that we need it at this moment, but I promise you, when it does happen, you will understand why it needed to be the way it ultimately unfolded. The more you open yourself to the love that connects you, the easier the connection will be made. As Rumi uttered so truthfully about the reality of life, "Love is the bridge between you and everything."[12]

Through my many years of working as a medium and having done hundreds of sittings in my life, I have learned many things about living from those who have crossed over. To begin with, suffering and loss belong to this world, not the world of spirit. As described before, when we leave this earth, we leave behind our physical bodies and along with it the pains, the losses, the grudges, and the anger, and it is why I know that nothing negative can come from the world of spirit. If anything, the spirit world wishes to direct us to the positive, loving, happy memories that they created here with their loved ones. The feelings of pain, loss, and separation that underpin all negative emotions do not exist in a place where survival is no longer threatened. Fear stems from the loss of self

---

12   M. J. Rumi and K. Helminski, *The Pocket Rumi* (Boulder, CO: Shambhala, 2008).

and individual annihilation. Those in the other world already experience connectedness, peace, and wholeness. Therefore, there is no need to let your life end because theirs transitioned to another part of the journey. I have never had a spirit communicator come forward and request that their loved one continue to focus on their death and loss. Instead, they let their loved ones know that they are closer to them now than ever before. They are okay and that they want their loved one to go on too. We can honor our loved ones in spirit by doing our best to continue our lives, living our lives to their fullest, and sharing the lives of those who have gone before with those who are still here.

Part 4

A Step-by-Step Approach to
Developing Mediumship

8

Begin by Working with the Power

Earlier in our journey together, we briefly touched upon the power and the important role it plays in mediumship. As we begin to move into the practical application of how to connect with the spirit world, it is important that we delve deeper into what the power is and how we know we are in it as well as learn a helpful practice to develop our power. Understanding the power is the backbone of all mediumistic work; therefore, if you take nothing else from this book, take this practice.

How Working with the Power Feels

As mentioned before in chapter 2, the power can feel different depending on which kind of mediumship is being practiced. Through learning to recognize these differences, you can learn to identify how the spirit world is wanting to work with you in that moment.

When working with mental mediumship, the power can feel like a rising or rapid sensation building within the medium and externally in the air around them. The atmosphere often begins to feel thick or electric. We can also feel a subtle sense of dissociation from the immediate physical space around us as our attention moves to our energetic awareness. As mediums move into the power, our senses become heightened and the air around us begins to feel more fluidlike or as if it has more density to it. It is in this space that we begin to sense and feel the presence of a spirit communicator.

When we are working in the trance states, the power feels quite the opposite of mental mediumship. Trance mediumship is a much more passive altered state of awareness, and the power reflects this. As the power comes, trance mediums often feel a sense of sleepiness, an inability to stay focused in the present moment, almost as if they are drifting into a semi sleepy state. The power often feels quite heavy, almost as if a lead or weighted blanket is being laid over you.

In healing, the power will feel different again. I have found that the healing power feels different to each person. Many experience it as a temperature change, heat or coolness. I personally experience it as a sense of coolness in the atmosphere; however, my hands begin to tingle and often become quite warm. Others feel tingling, buzzing, or thickening in the atmosphere around them. It all just depends on you and how it shows itself as you are sending healing energy.

In my experience with physical mediumship and physical phenomena, the power takes on a very dense quality. The atmosphere begins to feel incredibly thick and heavy with some sense of sleepiness. It can also feel as if there is energy being pulled from the solar plexus or as if the air around you feels quite viscous and fluid. There is also an acute awareness of the rise and fall of the energy, almost like waves that have peaks and valleys. At times the atmosphere can have a static electric feeling as well.

Why It's Important

It is important that a medium understands the power as it is more than just an energetic change. It has information within it and is the driving force in any kind of mediumistic work. The experience of the power almost acts like a guide in your communication. As you start to feel the power beginning to change around you, you know that there is a spirit presence there with you. Then, as you begin to focus your attention on where you feel the buildup of the energy, a spirit person begins to develop. This awareness of the change in the atmosphere gives you more information as you become more aware of the energetic difference moment to moment. For example, you may then begin to feel the essence of a male or a female standing next to you. This is coming from the experience of what is changing in the power. As it continues, it starts to change and take form even further. You may begin to feel an emotional connection to this presence, which then tells you that this is a friend or a relative. On and on, the power changes from moment to moment, and you gain more information from your experience until you are so well blended with the spirit's presence that it feels like you are becoming one. This is when you are fully in the power of the spirit.

The Power of the Spirit vs. Your Personal Power

When discussing working in or with the power, we are often discussing the power of the spirit specifically. This is the energetic change that comes upon us when we work with the spirit. However, there is another aspect of the power that is our own personal power, or aura. You can think about this as your energetic battery or divine spark that you bring to the table when making a link to the spirit. The more power that you have built up in your aura, the easier and clearer your link to the spirit world will be. Also, having a stronger personal power will support you in maintaining your link to the spirit world when your reading becomes challenging, or when tension or nerves enter your reading. Over time, by sitting in the power regularly, our personal power builds. It is vital for a medium to build their personal power to get clear, strong, and accurate information.

Our aura acts as the modulator of our mediumistic awareness. When we open up our aura, we are saying to the spirit world, "I am ready to connect with you." When we close down our aura, we are saying, "I'm no longer available to connect." Through learning how to work with our own aura and energetic power, we learn to gain control over our energy.

So how do we open and close our energy? We do this with two things: intent and how we focus. When we intend to open our aura, we also open our energetic awareness and become sensitive to the atmosphere around us. Energy follows thought, so intention is the first step.

It should be noted that intention and will are two very different mindsets. It is very easy to mistake will for intent, so let me define this a little further. Intention is open and relaxed. It's like a suggestion. To give you a visual, I like to think of this as an open palm facing upward. The open palm provides a loose structure of the possibility for whatever we are intending to occur. Will, on the other hand, is like a closed fist. It is forceful, directive, and makes things happen. We want to avoid willing our energy to move or to open. We merely need to intend that, if it's possible or when it's ready, our energy will naturally open up on its own. Don't force it. Intend and then let go of a desire for an outcome. Just relax and wait for a sensation to indicate something has changed.

However, intent is not enough. The second component is a soft or relaxed focus. If we are mentally trying to open our energy through imaginative visualization or willpower, our energy will not budge. This is because tension or effort inhibits energetic dilation. What opens our energy is surrendering and relaxing. When we surrender and relax, our energy responds. You can think of surrendering as having a relaxed, diffused focus that dilates our energy, while having a hard or specific focus contracts our energy. When we are wanting to open our energy, we want to relax so that it opens wide. You will know your energy is opening up because you will begin to feel bodily sensations of tingling, buzzing, warmth, heaviness, or thickness in the atmosphere, temperature changes, or numbness in the body. These subtle indicators tell you that you are becoming more energetically sensitive rather than physically focused in the mind.

One of the hardest things for students to learn to do is not try to control and make their energy do what they are aiming for. In all other areas of our life, we are taught that to do well, you must try to make it happen. Mediumship and working with your energy is the exact opposite. To be able to become sensitive and feel your own energy, you have to let go, surrender, become indifferent about the outcome, and allow. This is not something we are taught in our society. In fact, for some people, the idea of "surrendering" can be very uncomfortable or even frightening. For those of us who have had to control our environment to protect ourselves at a young age, surrender can feel very vulnerable and unfamiliar. If you find yourself in this category, know that this is okay and through slow and gentle practice, you will learn that letting go of control is safe and often quite freeing. Be patient with yourself and let yourself become comfortable little by little.

The reason we need to learn to let go of control is because this is how we start to become receptive and thereby able to sense when the spirit draws near—when something begins to happen *to* us rather than coming *from* us. When we want to start to sense and perceive the spirit, we need to let go of control so that we can notice what changes in our energy and the space around us. Far too often, students who are too eager to have an experience end up imagining or making up an experience rather than waiting for something genuine coming from spirit to occur. By learning to surrender, be patient, and wait for an atmospheric or energetic change to take place, we are training our awareness to follow the lead of the spirit rather than our imagination. This is the beginning of what we call "mind control," or learning to control the reactiveness or overactivity of the mind. This is critical to true mediumistic ability.

Sitting In the Power

What is sitting in the power? The simplest way to think about this practice is you are sitting in the energetic power of your own energy and then inviting the power of spirit—in this case, your guides and/or the Great Spirit—to be with you. Simple enough, right? But this practice actually is doing a lot more for your development than it may seem. By sitting in the power, we become familiar with what our energy feels like. This is important later on when we start making a link to spirit presences. When we know what our energy feels like, we can then easily identify when another presence steps into our energy. Also, sitting in the power will help us build our own energy reserves that we will use whenever we are working in any mediumistic capacity. It does not matter what kind of mediumship you are doing: when connecting with the spirit world, you will be using power to maintain that connection. The more power you have, the stronger the connection you will be able to make. Sitting in the power will also support us in becoming sensitive to feeling the power of the spirit. As mentioned before, this is the presence we feel when the spirit world draws near. The more we can identify and feel into the power of the spirit, the stronger the link we will create, and thereby the more accurate our information will be. Ultimately, sitting in the power can be viewed as creating a sacred space to commune with your spirit helpers. We are not trying to make a link with a spirit communicator; rather, we are coming to the spirit world and saying, "I'm just here. Do what you need to do to develop me. This is your time."

Everyone will experience sitting in the power differently, but people commonly report experiencing sensations similar to the energetic sensations I mentioned before. Buzzing, tingling, pressure on the neck or body, the sense of being wrapped up or held in a bubble, a sense of well-being and peace: these are all commonly experienced sensations along the energetic journey of sitting in the power. Basically, it's a change in your awareness and the atmosphere around you. As you relax into these sensations, the experience unfolds and deepens. When we experience these feelings and continue to relax past them, we move into a place of stillness and quiet within. This is sitting in the power.

Sitting in the power is the single most important practice a medium or psychic can do if they want to develop and improve their abilities. It helps us in three ways.

First, it teaches us to quiet and still the mind. To become receptive, we must learn to allow our mind to quiet and not become reactive to everything we experience. In the beginning, most students struggle with sitting in the power when their mind ends up reacting to every sensation or experience they have. Their minds immediately respond with, "What was that? What does it mean? What is happening?" Everything ends up having to have some kind of significance. This keeps the mind engaged and takes the medium out of the passive and receptive state we are trying to cultivate.

To break this habit, when you are sitting and something catches your attention, learn to notice it without trying to figure out its significance or do something with it mentally. Once it has been noticed, just take note of it. For example, let's say that while sitting, I begin to feel tingling in my hands and arms. Instead of allowing my mind to immediately say, "Oh wow! I feel this tingling. What is this? Is this my guide? Is this a spirit?" try to allow yourself to just take note of it. "Oh, my arms are tingling; great." Then just let it become part of the experience and let it go. Each time you experience a new sensation or experience, just take note of it and then let it go. Eventually, instead of mentally reacting to our experiences, we learn to notice, accept, and let it go. The less your mind reacts to the experiences you are having, the more you will cultivate the ability to maintain your passive, soft focus while allowing experiences to happen to you. This will keep you connected and keep your mind from engaging the experience, which will cause it to shut off. If you find that whenever you begin to sense sensations, they begin to fade as soon as you notice them, you are likely paying too much attention to them and your mind is engaging. Just go back to relaxing and focusing on the breath until they return.

Secondly, through this process of notice, accept, and let it go, sitting in the power teaches our mind to become passive and receptive. Living in the modern age, our minds are always looking for the next stimulus. We're always looking for something to do or for something to entertain us. Social media, the constant barrage of ads vying for your attention, the list of things to do in our minds—there can never be a moment where something is not going on. Sitting in the power helps train our mind to become still and develop passivity. When we become passive, we then can become receptive, and this is how we begin to notice the subtle energies that exist around us. The spirit world resides in these subtle energies and our receptivity and sensitivity allow the subtlety to become much more obvious.

Lastly, sitting in the power gives our guides and helpers who work with us the opportunity to develop us. While classes and workshops are helpful in practicing making a link and delivering information, it is the time outside of class where we give our spirit helpers the opportunity to work on us energetically that truly develops our spiritual senses. I'm a strong believer that it is our spirit helpers who develop us. Whenever we devote time to our spiritual helpers, I always imagine them like little scientists in white lab coats and a clipboard looking at my energy and saying, "Okay, what can we adjust in Michael's energy today?" It is through their energetic work that they open our clairvoyance, our clairaudience, our clairsentience, and our claircognizance. All we have to do is give them time to do so and learn to get out of the way.

Every great medium of the past and today still sits in the power regularly as a means of continuing their development, both mediumistically and spiritually. You can liken this mental training to the flexibility of a muscle. If you keep stretching and allowing your awareness to move in and out of an energetically sensitive state more often, connecting becomes so much easier. It keeps our awareness flexible and makes connecting with the spirit world stronger and clearer. Even if you're not wanting to become a medium or psychic, understanding the power can help you with other spiritual practices or skills that require your mind to be quiet and still so that a flow can occur. Sitting in the power is the most important practice for connecting within.

How It Differs from Meditation

I am often asked how sitting in the power is different from regular meditation. This will all depend on what kind of meditation you do. If you are practicing a type of meditation where your mind is active, such as visualizations, contemplation, or mindfulness, we are staying mentally actively engaged to some degree. Other forms of meditation that encourage a stilling of the mind and no thought are much closer to sitting in the power. Another component that I find to be different is the intent. When sitting in the power, our intent is to sense and expand our energy so that we feel it externally around us. Then we invite the presence of the divine to join us and remain in a still and quiet place. It is more about the communion of our soul with the divine within and without rather than a more mentally active state.

Additionally, it should be noted that when we are sitting in the power, we are not trying to make a connection to a loved one in spirit or actively seek information from our guides. Our goal when sitting is moving into a still, quiet place within. When we look at any major religion, we will always see that they contain some kind of stilling or quieting practice. Whether deep prayer, deep meditation, or other trance-inducing state, we are told that the voice of God is found in the stillness—as in the phrase "the still, small voice of God." By cultivating stillness of the mind, we truly learn receptivity and can have incredibly powerful experiences of oneness with our own spiritual nature and a much bigger sense of the divine.

EXERCISE
Sitting In the Power

I am often asked how long one should sit in the power. Well, that just depends on how much time you have. More sitting is better than not sitting, so do what works for you. If you can only do ten minutes, do that. If you can do thirty minutes or more, great. Ideally, you would work yourself up to an hour. The more you practice sitting, the easier it will become and the longer you will be able to maintain it. As for frequency, that will depend on what is comfortable for you. I often suggest if you can do it every day, that is ideal. However, not everyone can or likes to. If every day is too much, I would suggest a minimum of four times a week for at least thirty minutes each time. This is the minimum frequency I have noticed where people make steady development. If four times a week is still too much, once a week will suffice. But if you decide to do it once a week, make it a very special and important appointment with the other world. By viewing it as your weekly communion with the spirit world, you are creating a much stronger impact in your development and dedication to becoming a medium. However long you decide to do, make it consistent.

To begin this practice, you will want to find a relaxed and comfortable position. I recommend you do it sitting up because most people have an association between lying down and sleeping. Find a comfortable chair that supports your back, is comfortable on your bottom, and allows your feet to touch the floor easily. You will be sitting in this position for anywhere between ten minutes and an hour, so it is important that you are comfortable and can maintain this position without any of your limbs falling asleep for the duration of the sitting. Try not to have your feet tucked under you or crossed unless your body allows this comfortably. Once you find a comfortable position, try to maintain the same position through the entire time of the sitting. The less you move, the better. A still body encourages a still mind. If you find that you feel odd sensations like tickling on your face or the need to scratch your nose, try not to do it. Oftentimes these are energetic sensations, and to move would disrupt them. Do your best to notice, accept, and relax past them. Most times they will dissipate on their own. If it becomes unbearable, though, go ahead and scratch it.

As you move into this meditative state, we are aiming for a relaxed but aware state of mind. We do not want to fall asleep, although if you do, you probably needed the nap anyway. If you do find that you begin to doze off, bring your awareness back to the breath and use this as your anchor throughout. If you need to bring yourself back consciously a bit more, wiggle your fingers or move your toes to keep you from slipping too deep into a sleepy state. Also note that when thoughts and feelings arise, which I promise you they will, just allow yourself to move your awareness back to the breath. Do not fight it or become frustrated with the thoughts that come and go. The goal is to notice them, accept them, and then let them go. Try not to engage them or follow them; just gently acknowledge and accept them as part of the experience. Acceptance is key throughout. Allow yourself to accept the thoughts that come and then just gently allow them to pass like clouds in the sky.

Note that sitting in the power should not be a highly visual practice. Many students are quick to want to see pictures, colors, and images, but this is not what we want to cultivate. What is more important is what you feel. Notice, accept, and let go of the sensations that occur while you are sitting. If images arise, they are most likely from your thinking mind needing to give you something to do. It is very easy for the mind to make up images; it is much harder to make up feelings. Therefore, relax and notice what you feel rather than what you see, especially in the beginning of this practice. Humans are visual creatures, and our thinking mind will always try to give you a picture for what you are feeling. Try not to pay too much attention to these visuals. Again, mediumship is the art of feeling. Stillness is the goal of sitting in the power.

Be patient with yourself. You will likely have plenty of monkey mind. That is okay. This is why sitting in the power is called a practice. In general, it usually takes about ten minutes for the mind to settle down for most people. It takes time, practice, and training to get good at sitting in the power; however, once you do, it will open the door to so much more in the way of your spiritual gifts and awareness. This skill is really the backbone of what it is to work mediumistically or psychically. You can download the guided audio version of this meditation on my website. See recommended resources for the meditations link.

Become comfortable wherever you're sitting. Allow yourself to begin to connect with the breath. Notice the inhale and the exhale, not intervening in any way. Just observing your breathing. Let your thoughts find their natural place of rest.

Gently bring your awareness to the central part of your being, the part of yourself that is connected to the divine spark within. Allow yourself to begin to feel into that space. As you feel into this space, experience and intend an expansion from within. Allow it to move and surround your being so that you become aware of the space in front of you and behind you, below you and above, on your left and your right. It's as if the atmosphere around you becomes an extension of you. Allow yourself to feel into this space.

As you feel into this space, with your next breath, allow yourself to become aware of a white light either above or in front of you. Don't worry if you don't see it; just feel and know that it's there. This white light very easily moves through you, surrounds you, and lifts you, making you feel lighter and brighter, lighter and brighter, lighter and brighter. So light and so bright, you allow your awareness to move up, up, up into a higher space in your awareness. So light and so bright, your awareness easily moves into this higher space in your mind and you feel the peace this brings you.

Allow yourself some time to sit in this stillness and quiet and feel the presence and the space around you. Should thoughts or feelings arise, let them act like clouds passing in the sky.

Rest in this space. Let yourself stay here as long as you can.

When you're feeling the energy beginning to dissipate, allow yourself to reconnect with the breath. Thank those you have worked with during this time as you gently allow your breath to become deeper—each inhale bringing you back to your normal awareness breath by breath, moment by moment. Don't rush it.

Whenever you feel back in your body and fully return, you can open your eyes.

Hopefully you feel a bit more relaxed, calm, and centered. You may have felt sensations such as tingling, buzzing, warmth, heaviness, lightness, expansiveness, a sense of shrinking, or all of the above. This is completely normal. If you felt nothing, don't worry! This is why we call sitting in the power a practice. The more you do it, the easier it will become and the better at it you'll get. As this is the single most important practice you can do to develop your mediumship, you will do it many times and it will eventually get easier and easier. Keep at it and you will discover the peace, joy, and profound experiences that can come from this practice.

9

Making Sense of the Sensations You Experience

Now that you have been practicing sitting in the power, hopefully daily, the next step in our journey is to begin making sense of the sensations that you experience. It is likely that while sitting in the power, at some point you have felt tingling, buzzing, warmth, heaviness, lightness (sometimes at the same time), or perhaps a thickening of the atmosphere. These are all examples of the ways in which we can experience our own energy.

Attunement

Becoming sensitive to the energy and atmosphere around us is the goal of our work so far. Being able to pay attention to subtle energetic changes in the space around us will help us better recognize and discern what is our energy versus not. We become sensitive by relaxing our awareness and not trying to make something happen or force an experience. By being present in the moment and noticing what catches our attention, we will naturally begin to enter a more sensitive state. This process is called "attunement." Attunement occurs when we move from our normal state of awareness to a more sensitive state where we are then able to make sense of the subtle sensations that happen to us and around us. Before doing any kind of work with the spirit world, we will always begin with attunement. You will know that you have achieved this state because the sensations will guide you. The more you can feel these energetic shifts in the atmosphere, the more attuned you are becoming.

EXERCISE
Attunement Process

Becoming comfortable wherever you're sitting, allow yourself to begin to connect with the breath. Notice the inhale and the exhale, and do not try to control your breathing. Let your breath breathe you. You can do this by noticing what your breath does if you do absolutely nothing. As you breathe, allow your thoughts to find their natural place of rest.

When you're ready, gently bring your awareness to the central part of your being. This is the part of yourself that is connected to the divine spark that exists within you. Allow yourself to begin to feel into that space. As you feel into this space, experience and intend an expansion from within. Allow it to move and surround your being so that you become aware of the space in front of you and behind you, below and above you, on your left and your right. It's as if the atmosphere around you becomes an extension of you. Allow yourself to feel into the space around you. When you begin to feel tingling, buzzing, or a thickness in the atmosphere, you know you are attuned. When you're ready, you can gently open your eyes and see how well you can maintain the awareness of the tingling, buzzing, and thickness of the atmosphere.

If you noticed that this process sounds familiar, that's because it is! The attunement process is the beginning part of sitting in the power, except now instead of moving deeper into the stillness and the quiet, we are sensitive and ready to move into whatever kind of connection we want to make with the spirit. Whether it's a healing session, trance sitting, psychic reading, or mental mediumship reading, it will all begin with the attunement process. It is our launching pad into our energetic sensitivity and spiritual awareness.

Narration

Once you have become attuned, then you are able to begin connecting with a spirit presence. As you do this, the energy will begin to change around you. The sensations that you experience will act as your guide along the journey of the communication. The best way to allow the sensations to guide you through this process is to simply describe what you are feeling as it is happening. This is called narration. The key here is to not stop to think about what you are experiencing, but rather continuously describe what you are experiencing as it happens. You can think of this like you are looking out a moving car window and describing things as they pass. You don't stop to focus on a single sign or building; if you did, you would miss something. Rather, you continuously describe what you are seeing as it moves past you. You repeat this process as the scenery changes. This describes exactly how we work with the impressions that come to us from the spirit presence. We do not stop to think about them or figure out what they mean, we just narrate. Learning to narrate your experience without over-focusing is essential to your mediumistic development.

Our ability to narrate our experience is directly related to our ability to stay passive without our mind disrupting the process. It is in this part of our development that we must start to notice what we do mentally that engages our thinking mind. You will find that when our mind is engaged, it will decrease these sensations. When we are relaxed or indifferent, the sensations increase. For example, if I notice that I am beginning to feel a particular sensation, and then my mind quickly thinks "What was that?", I will likely notice that I begin to lose the sensation. Conversely, when I (1) notice a sensation, (2) relax into it, (3) accept it, and (4) then let it go, I find that the sensation may increase. Being aware of our ability to maintain a passive awareness rather than a reactive awareness will help us sustain a strong link with the other world.

EXERCISE

Practicing Narration

Allow yourself to become still and quiet by taking several gentle breaths and letting your thoughts find their natural place of rest. As the mind begins to quiet, allow yourself to gently bring your awareness to the central part of your being. This can be in either your heart space or your solar plexus or wherever you sense it is for you. As you feel into this divine connection within, allow yourself to wait for a stirring within your being. Do not force anything to happen, just intend that an opening from within this power may begin when it is ready. Intend that it might move to fill the body—let this take as long as it needs, at least several breaths.

Allow the subtle sense of this expansion to begin expanding beyond the body. Let this take as long as it takes to feel this shift. Relax into the atmosphere, allowing your energy to expand and fill the space in front of you, behind you, on your left and your right, and above you. It is as if nerve endings move from your body into the atmosphere around you. Feel into the air and the space around you, relaxing even more.

When you can feel the atmosphere around you changing, intend that your energy will expand even further—each inhale expanding the energy, each exhale relaxing deeper. As you relax, intend that your energy might expand to fill the room in which you sit. Again, do not force this or just imagine it. When you are in this space, let yourself sit in it for a while, taking note of the subtle changes that occur. You may begin to feel tingling, warmth, heaviness, lightness, numbness, thickening of the atmosphere—notice this, accept it, and then relax more.

After sitting in this energy for some time, see if you can describe out loud what you are feeling without losing the sensations. If you find that you are losing the sensations, allow yourself to relax back into the experience and let yourself go. Otherwise, see if you can notice the changes that occur as you describe what is happening to you.

When you feel that you are ready, you can begin to reconnect with your breath and return to your normal awareness.

Take Time for Reflection

Write down what you noticed and what helped you experience more sensations. What diminished them? What did you feel? What sensations were the strongest? What helped you maintain the sensitivity while you were speaking?

In the narration exercise, we practiced attunement and narrating what we were sensing and feeling. Thus, we focused on becoming sensitive and simply noticing. I often describe this to my students as becoming a little nerve ending that describes whatever stimulus is happening to it. At this stage in our development, it isn't important for you to get specific details of any kind. We are merely learning how to sense the atmosphere around us and accurately describe what we can. This is called having energetic awareness—we are becoming more aware of energy and what it feels like.

However, it is important that we learn to become familiar with our own energy first. As you become increasingly familiar with your own energy, you can begin to develop a baseline before working with the spirit world. When we begin to work with spirit presences, whether it be guides in the next chapter or loved ones in spirit after that, we must notice how our baseline energy changes as a spiritual presence enters into the space. This is how we develop discernment between what is our energy versus what isn't.

The beginning of genuine spirit communication starts with your own ability to become sensitive. As I mentioned before, we become sensitive to the atmosphere around us and use the earlier sensations (tingling, buzzing, etc.) as a marker that we have arrived in an attuned state. Then, depending on what we are trying to connect with—a guide or a departed loved one—we will offer our intent for them to step into our energy. As the spirit draws near, you may begin to feel a shift in the power around you. This can feel like pressure on the back of your neck, the feeling of someone standing next to you, or some centralized portion of the air around you becoming pressurized or thick. This is where you would begin to narrate your experience. For example, if I started to feel a pressure on the right side of my body, I would simply state aloud, "I'm beginning to feel a pressure on the right-hand side of me."

As I feel this pressure, it may start to change. Now I may begin to feel the energy ramp up, and as it does, I get a sense of excitement within me. "As I feel this pressure to my right, it begins to ramp up. As it ramps up, I start to feel a sense of excitement coming from this energy." As the energy and sensations change once more, I will repeat this process of narration. As you follow the experience sensation by sensation, eventually it will become more specific and become a descriptor of your spirit communicator. We will explore this more in chapter 11 when we learn to make a link with the spirit world. It is important to remember that the sensations may be very subtle or not totally obvious at first. This will develop over time and is cultivated through the practice of sitting in the power.

10

Connecting with Your Spirit Guides

Developing a relationship with your spirit guides is a very special part of your mediumship journey. When we look back at the spirit guides who have brought through such great information for us here on this side of life, we recognize the special relationship that connecting with your spirit helpers can bring.

Some well-known spirit guides include Silver Birch, who was the guide for Maurice Barbanell and who brought through beautiful philosophies about life. One of my personal favorite quotes from Silver Birch appears at the beginning of this book; again, it is:

> There is no joy and no service that can match helping others. In a world so full of darkness, where millions have lost their way, where there are countless numbers troubled and perplexed with sorrow in their hearts, who awake each morning in fear and apprehension of what the day brings—if you can help one soul to find some serenity and to realize that he/she is not neglected, but surrounded by arms of infinite love, that is a great work. It is more important than anything else.[13]

Spirit guides can inspire us to live in a better, more harmonious way. They are our faithful companions as we develop our mediumship and as

---

13   M. Barbanell, Silver Birch books, http://www.silverbirchpublishing.co.uk /books.php (accessed January 24, 2022).

we evolve as a spirit. Cultivating this relationship can bring about beautiful partnerships that can create miracles.

One such partnership was between George Chapman and his guide, Dr. Lang. Through this relationship, Dr. Lang was able to perform beautiful trance healing through his medium, which was thoroughly documented throughout Chapman's healing career. What makes this match-up even more special is how it not only showed evidence for the reality of spirit guides, but it simultaneously provided physical healing, demonstrating the power spirit can have in a very physical way in our lives if we let it.

Personally, I did not know who worked with me for a large portion of my spiritual development. It is not important that you know who your guides are to be able to work with them or to develop as a medium. However, it is a beautiful relationship that we can cultivate and begin to develop early in our unfoldment of our spiritual awareness.

What Is a Spirit Guide?

A guide is a spirit being who works with you to help you on your spiritual journey. Spirit guides are your spiritual support from the other side of life. If you can think of yourself as the pilot of your life, your spirit guide is like your ground control guiding you into landing. They help you achieve the spiritual goals and lessons you planned to learn in this life. Spirit guides can also work with you on specific tasks, such as trance, art, or spiritual teaching.

While some people have many guides who help them with different tasks, others have a single guide who helps them with all things. It is not important how many guides you have. As long as you have support helping you from the spirit world, that is what is important. Certain guides can work with you for a temporary amount of time or throughout your whole life. Generally, each medium will have a main guide who acts as the central figure who is your go-to for most things. This guide is usually with you from birth, but many people do not become aware of them until later in life.

I am often asked if beings like angels, ascended masters, aliens, and even deities such as Jesus or Mary can be your spirit guide. Personally, I want to have some kind of validation or evidence to support that my guide is who they say they are. While validation that your guide is who they say they are is not important, it can be helpful. While angels, ascended masters, aliens, and deities can be helpers on your journey, I would encourage you to see if there is someone else there working with you that might be more specifically tailored to you.

It is common for our minds to want to create an image or an idea of who our guide is. This is why you commonly saw Native American and East Asian guides throughout the history of Western mediumship. This is because at the time, these groups of people were romanticized as seeming more in tune with the natural world and more spiritually advanced. The mind of the medium can often try to create an image for our guide that we feel the most comfortable with. This is why I do not put too much emphasis on who our guides are. This is not to say that you cannot receive evidence about who your guide is if they lived a physical existence. To the contrary, it can be quite powerful when we receive validatable evidence that confirms our guide is who they say they are.

My Experience of Meeting My Guide

I was well into my development as a psychic and medium before I had the privilege of meeting my guide. For many years, I wondered why I hadn't had the experience of knowing who was there. I knew *something* was working with me; I just never had an awareness of who it was. This never bothered me, but I was curious why I hadn't yet made this connection.

I was at an interesting place in my development during this time. I was very involved with the New Age perspective of spiritual development and felt that I was not receiving the proof or the evidence I was seeking.

Sure, I had had amazing experiences with the spirit world, but none of it ever truly convinced me that I was in a personal relationship with the spirit world. I could give a reading, but I wanted something more for myself.

I remember coming across a video of a spiritualist medium giving a talk about his journey and experience with connecting with his guide. He had been sitting in a physical mediumship circle for a year with no results. On the last night of sitting in the circle, he decided that he would give up after this night if nothing happened. As the evening went on, nothing occurred. Resigned that he would not continue his development, just as they were about to turn on the light and end the session, the medium was told by a clairaudient voice to continue to sit. As soon as he did, a spirit presence blended with him and dramatically began to address the group through his voice. This began his years of development and connection to the spirit world.

I remember watching this video and felt very intrigued and inspired by this story. Surely, if the spirit world could be that obvious and clear with this medium, they could do the same with me. So I sat down and said, "Okay, spirit. I'm going to just sit here in the silence and wait for you. I don't care how long it takes, and I'm going to put aside everything I think I know and just wait for you. If you come, great; if you don't, also great. But if you can do that for him, I know you can do that for me." So I set up a seat in my closet and turned on a red light. This began a series of sittings in the stillness and the quiet. I came to the experience without any agenda or desire. This, I feel, was the most important part. It allowed me to just be present with whatever would occur without desire or expectation.

That first night I sat, nothing happened. The next night nothing happened. I continued doing this for about a week, and then one evening my head began to move slight from being centrally positioned to leaning over my left shoulder. It felt as though it was moving on its own. I did not think too much of it and just noticed it, accepted it, and let it go. Then, at the end of the session, my head would move back to the central position. After the first night this happened, it would happen each time I sat. At that point I figured it must be something to do with spirit.

Another week went by and this same pattern with my head continued. Then, one night, once my head moved to the left, I suddenly felt tingles moving from right to left across my shoulder and down my chest. Then my head began to move back to the center again and I was returned to normal awareness. I thought this was a rather interesting development, but I just took note of it and let it go. This pattern of the head movement followed by the tingles continued for another couple of weeks. Then, one evening, just after my head moved to the left, I suddenly heard clairaudiently to my right, loud and clear, "Paging Dr. White! Paging Dr. White!"[14] Immediately following the clairaudient experience, the tingles rushed in from right to left across my shoulder and down my chest.

"Oh! So your name is Dr. White!" I was surprised and shocked but also excited. Something had happened completely unexpectedly and coincided with the sensations I had been feeling for weeks. I remember sending this thought to the presence: "What is your first name?" and I heard "Peter." Being the strong-minded person I was at that point, I thought, "This isn't weird enough—it's way too common. Give me something weirder." It was then that I thought up the name "Felix" and was satisfied with its uniqueness.

Over the next couple of months, as I continued to sit, I would occasionally receive out of nowhere some bit of information. I received the year 1952, that he was connected to Oxford, England, and that he was a psychologist by profession and had spent much of his career studying consciousness, religion, and philosophy. There was other information that he gave over the months and I took note of it each time he would come through.

---

14 A pseudonym for privacy purposes.

One day, I was sitting at a computer and I suddenly felt an overwhelming urge to look him up using the information I had gathered over the months. I typed into Google "Felix White psychologist." Nothing came up. I felt slightly defeated but quickly recalled that he had given me a different name first. I typed in "Peter White psychologist" and the very first hit was his first and last name with the word *psychologist* next to it. I clicked it and saw the year he had passed away was 1952. As I read more, I saw that he had studied the mind and consciousness and that he had worked at Oxford as a psychologist. To say I was blown away was an understatement! Here was all the information I had been given, easily and perfectly matching this individual. As I continued to read, I was even more amazed when I read that he was a member of the Society for Psychical Research and had sat and studied mediums, including physical mediums, which is the kind of mediumship I was sitting to develop! At that point, my jaw dropped and I was very moved by the experience.

Finally, after all this time of development, waiting, and sitting for the spirit, I had received evidential proof that I had a guide and that he was truly working with me. I genuinely believe that the success of this connection came from my ability to put aside what I thought I knew, set aside my expectations, my desires, and become open and still. Since that point of development, I am happy to say the relationship has grown and developed over the years, and he still works with me in the trance states.

———

While my experience was meaningful for me, this is not needed to develop your mediumship or connect with your guide. Instead, I share this story to illustrate what is possible when we learn to surrender, trust in spirit, and meet the spirit world without expectations or a desire for an outcome.

What is important is being able to identify when our guides are drawing near to us. By developing a way to sense and feel when our guides draw near to us, we are able to begin developing a relationship with them. It is through *feeling* our guide that they can learn to communicate with us in a real and tangible way. The common expectation is that our guide will appear to us in some visual or intense or obvious way, and when they do, they will impart some kind of great revelation upon us. This is not how it works. Can it happen? Yes. But more often than not, we experience our guides in a similar way that we experience the spirit world: subtly at first until we cultivate our sensitivity, making the subtle much more obvious.

It is also important to share that I almost never reach out to my guide and say, "Hey, can you do this for me or give me this answer?" I do not believe this is the most efficient way of working with your spirit helpers. Instead, develop the ability to notice and feel when your guide comes to you rather than you going to them. Essentially, your guide is not here to fix every trouble you have or answer every question you have. A guide is here to support you in your journey when the time is right. This is why it is so important to learn to sense when your guide is drawing near to you. In most instances, the times that we connect with our guide will be at the end of meditation or time that we set aside for them. This is an important practice to get into because it offers them time to connect and blend with you. However, there are few instances outside of that where your guide will make themselves known. In the rare instance that they do, you should stop, become passive, and sense what your guide is bringing you. This is not a common occurrence, hence why when it does happen, I consider it and it stands out to me. Otherwise, my guide is there when I am working and the rest of the time I'm just not aware of them.

What Guides Do vs. What They Don't Do

Before we dive deeper into how we can sense and feel our guide, I believe it is important to understand what guides do versus what they do not do.

What guides do:

- » Support you in meeting your spiritual and personal development goals

- » Help you in your readings and mediumship development

- » Inspire you through spiritual impressions and insights

- » Work with you in the trance states for philosophy, healing, and evidential mediumship

- » Occasionally let you know when there is something important to pay attention to

- » Help you cultivate kindness, compassion, and personal growth

- » Unconditionally love and support you

What guides do not do:

- » Give you answers to all your problems

- » Suggest what you should eat, how to dress, or what to buy

- » Give you winning lotto numbers

- » Scare, intimidate, or test you

- » Trick you or punish you

- » Dictate how you should live your life

- » Become angry or annoyed with you

I feel it is important for students to learn that our guides do not provide any kind of retribution or judgment for our lives or our actions. This is our story we are playing out; they are there on the sidelines to help us if need be. But from a spiritual perspective, everything we do in this life is about learning. We just get to learn it the hard way or the simpler way. Either way, it is learning. Our guides recognize this and do not have an attachment to the outcome. They just want to support us the best they can.

Through developing your connection to your guide, you are creating a relationship that will be with you the rest of your life. A spirit friend and companion will always do their best to provide you with guidance and root for you from their side of life. I hope you will meet them with an open heart, without expectation or desire, and a willingness to let them unfold your spiritual gifts and potential. With patience and openness, who knows what is possible?

Learning to Sense and Feel Your Guide

As we move into this next exercise, this will be the first time that we are inviting a spiritual presence into our energy. We will allow ourselves to become sensitive (becoming the nerve ending) and then invite the presence of our helper to join us. Do not worry if nothing happens or you do not experience anything. The first several times you do this exercise, there is no expectation that you will notice anything. However, there are best practices that will support you in this exercise.

Be sure that when you come to this exercise, let go of any expectations that it needs to feel, look, or be any specific way. The less expectation that you have going into it, the more neutral you can be and the more likely you will experience something. It is the act of searching or trying that creates tension and thereby inhibits the potential to experience. I often suggest to my students to be okay with getting nothing. The more we are able to accept nothing happening, the less likely our mind will try to step in and fill in the experience. If we can come to the spirit world with an open mind, an open heart, and a willingness to step out of the way, we can often have incredible experiences. The hard part is letting go of a desire for an outcome and the expectation that something specific should happen. Just come to the spirit and say, "I'm going to just sit here and wait. If something happens, great! If nothing happens, great!" If you treat both outcomes with the same level of interest, your awareness will be more receptive. If nothing happens this time, try it again another time.

Beginning by breathing, allow yourself to find a comfortable position that works for you, sitting upright with hands resting in your lap. Become aware of the gentle rhythm of your breathing; as you do this, allow your thoughts to find their natural place of rest. Let go of any expectations, desires, or distractions. If anything does distract you, gently bring your awareness back to the breath.

Notice the inhale and the exhale as you sit in this space. Gently bring your awareness to the central part of your being—that space that is the divine spark within you. As you feel into this space, allow it to begin expanding with your intent and let a sense of peace and love fill you as you do. Wait for a sense of expansion from within and allow this energy to fill the body. When it is ready, allow it to expand beyond the body so that you become aware of what's in front of you and behind you, below you and above you, on your left and on your right.

Take note of what your power and energy feels like that surrounds you now. What sensations do you feel? What does the atmosphere feel like? What does your body feel like? This is you in your own energy; what does it feel like? Allow yourself to passively notice and observe as you become comfortable in this space. Stay passive and neutral, without any expectations of what is to come. Just notice what your energy is like right now.

With your energy expanded and open, send a thought out to your guide who works with you and invite them to step close into your energy so that you might become aware of what they feel like. Ask them to give you a sensation that lets you know they are there, asking once and then just waiting. Don't worry if you don't feel it right away; just stay neutral and wait.

Take note of any slight changes that may have occurred or any sensations that may have changed. With your next breath, send another thought out that your guide might step even closer to you and give you whatever sign or signature they wish to give. Ask once and then observe.

Take note of what you felt. If you felt nothing, that is okay. Just stay neutral and passive. One last time, invite your guide to begin to step even closer, giving you a sign or sensation that it is them. Ask once and then just wait.

Take note of anything you felt or experienced. With your next breath, thank your guide for being with you, whether you felt something or not, and for this time as they begin to withdraw their energy. As they withdraw, notice if you feel any change in your energy.

Once you feel that you have returned to your own energy, you can begin to adjust your breathing to take nice full breaths as you return to normal awareness. When you are fully ready to return, open your eyes.

Take note of this entire experience. Write things down that you experienced so that you can compare it to the next time you do this exercise.

11

Connecting with Spirit Communicators

In the last chapter, we explored how to connect with your spirit guide. Through becoming sensitive, we were able to sense and feel another presence stepping into our energy. Now we will take this one step further and sense and feel the presence of a spirit communicator. Connecting with a spirit person is very similar to each step we have covered along the way. First we become sensitive through attuning our awareness to the atmosphere around us. Then we offer the intent that a spirit presence might begin to step into our energy. In the last chapter we invited a spirit guide, but in this chapter we will invite the presence of a loved one in spirit (our own if you are practicing this alone or your partner's if you are practicing this with someone else). This process is very similar in that we blend with the presence and allow them to impress us. As we are impressed by the spirit communicator, we will narrate what we are experiencing, as we did in chapter 9. Let us explore the structure of a reading and how a connection with a spirit communicator works.

Structure of a Reading

The structure of a reading leading up to the link with the spirit world is generally the same. By becoming aware of how a reading generally unfolds, we know what to expect and our ability to easily fall into the flow of the reading is increased. In general, the prep work for a reading begins prior to the sitter's arrival. In the beginning of your development, this time may be as short as ten minutes to as long as forty (as it was for me in the beginning of my journey). During this time you are centering yourself and letting go of your day. You are quieting the mind and beginning to engage your passive awareness. For some people, this will be a time for attunement or sitting in the power. I would not necessarily recommend sitting in the power right before a reading for some people as this can leave one too sleepy or passive. However, for others, this isn't a problem and it can help them become sensitive. Others like to listen to certain music that helps them lift their awareness to a more passive or inspired state. I've also known some people to watch other mediums' work (such as through videos online) to get their awareness in the mode of reading. Whatever you decide to do, and however long it takes, I recommend taking some time to center yourself before your reading.

Opening Prayer

During this time I generally like to offer an opening prayer to my spirit helpers that supports me in getting into the right headspace for a reading. After all, without the help of my spirit helpers, none of this is possible. Your opening prayer can be as elaborate or as simple as you'd like. Everyone is different. For me, I like to keep everything with my mediumship simple. My opening prayer, which I have used for years, goes like this:

> *Great Spirit,*
> *Help me to get out of the way.*
> *Help me to follow your lead.*
> *Help me to surrender to you.*
> *I can't do this without you.*
> *Thank you.*

I like this opening prayer because it helps me get into the mindset of surrender. It helps me recognize that none of this would work without the help and leadership of my spirit helpers and the spirit world. It reminds me that there is nothing I have to accomplish; rather, I just follow along with whatever they bring me. Affirming that I can't do it without them helps me put all my trust in their very capable hands.

Attunement

Attunement can happen before or after your sitter arrives. I tend to prefer attuning before and after my sitter is with me. Before because it helps me become sensitive without a sense of a time crunch and I can fully move into a space of sensitivity. After because once my sitter is there, I want to attune to the power that will begin to move me in the moment. It is up to you how and when you want to start becoming sensitive to the spirit world. Sometimes it will happen to you on its own as you begin to get closer to the time of your reading. It is almost as if the spirit world is preparing you ahead of time. I notice this most before a demonstration.

Opening Spiel

Once your sitter arrives and you have greeted them warmly and openly, you will want to set the expectations for the reading. I refer to this segment as "the opening spiel." The opening spiel is important because it gives your sitter all the information they will need on how to behave, respond, and what to expect during the reading. Because there are so many different readers out there, all of whom work differently, it is important to do your opening for each person who comes to sit with you, whether they are seasoned sitters or it is their first reading.

After greeting the sitter warmly, I will ask, "Have you ever had a reading before?" I ask this because it informs me to what degree I need to go into detail about what to expect in the reading and how I want them to respond. For someone who has had many readings, it may not be as necessary to go into great detail. Letting them know how you work and how you want them to respond may be enough. For others, it may be helpful to explain how mediumship works, what your experience as a medium is like, and how you'd like them to respond. We do this because many people come with differing levels of understanding of how mediumship works. As mentioned previously, there are so many different expectations as to what a medium is and does and also what the experience is like for the medium. Some people think it is like talking on the phone and therefore have great expectations when they come into the sitting. Others may think that a psychic and a medium are the same thing. It is the job of the medium to educate the sitter as best they can prior to the reading. This helps avoid any issues ahead of time and tempers expectations of the sitter.

Below is my opening spiel, which begins after asking if they've ever had a reading before and the assumed answer is no:

> "Okay, great. I hope this will be a great first reading experience for you then. Do note that I may not look at you; I may look around you or off to the side. I may have my eyes closed at times. Know that this isn't personal, I am just paying attention to other experiences. Is this okay with you?"
>
> "Yes."
>
> "Thank you. Everyone who does this works differently, so I will share with you how I work to help you better understand what to expect. I am going to take a few minutes and begin to become sensitive to the atmosphere and the energy around me. As I do this, I am waiting for a sense of one of your loved ones to step forward. As I start to feel their presence, I will begin to describe what I am experiencing. I may experience it through feelings and sensations, emotions, through pictures and images, through sounds, or just a knowing internally. As I experience these impressions from your loved one, I will describe what I am experiencing. Hopefully as I describe what is happening, it will begin to sound like someone you know in spirit. If you can understand the information, just say yes. If you cannot understand it, say no. If you are not sure or you need more information, you can say you are not sure or you need more information. Try not to add anything beyond *yes*, *no*, and *I don't know*

because it will get me into my thinking mind, and I want to stay passive and receptive rather than trying to think about what I am getting. As I am describing this information to you, there is a good chance that I may have no idea what I am talking about. But as long as it makes sense to you, that's what's important. Does this make sense to you?"

"Yes."

"Great. I don't want you to tell me who, but was there someone in particular you were hoping to hear from today?"

"Yes."

"Okay, great. Do know that I cannot control who comes forward; however, in most instances, who you are hoping to hear from will come forward. It is also possible that who you are hoping to hear from won't be the first communicator. If this is the case, keep an open mind as oftentimes another communicator enters first to open the way, and then your hoped-for loved one will come. Does this make sense to you?"

"Yes."

"Okay, great. Do you have any questions for me about how this works, what to expect, or how I want you to respond?"

"No."

"Okay, awesome. Then give me a few minutes to quiet my mind, and I will let you know when I am ready to begin. Thank you."

Notice how I explain exactly what to expect, how I want my sitter to respond, and check in with them to make sure they have all their possible questions answered. The more we can clear up any misconception or confusion in the beginning, the less likely we will run into trouble as we move through the reading. Ultimately, both the sitter and the medium want this experience to be the best it can. Therefore, by setting the ground rules for how you work the best, the more likely a positive outcome will occur.

I will often also add to my spiel that every time I work with the spirit world in this way, it is an experiment. It may or may not work. In the case that it does not, I will always offer a reschedule or refund. Generally, any time I have rescheduled a reading because it wasn't flowing that day, it has worked the next time I read for them.

Whenever we do a reading, we always want to give information with a sense of sensitivity and an empathetic or caring demeanor. Sure, there can be levity in a reading, but ultimately you are dealing with people's loved ones who have passed. We want to always ensure that we are sensitive to the energy and emotion of the person that you are sitting with. At the beginning of the reading, make sure to be warm, friendly, and open. This will help your sitter relax. If you notice that they are tense, never be afraid to check in with them and ask, "How are you feeling right now? Is there anything I can answer for you that might make you more comfortable?" Remember, you are creating a safe space for your sitter. The more relaxed and receptive they are, the better.

Lastly, having a consistent opening spiel is very helpful in getting you into the power. Eventually this opening becomes almost mindless to repeat, and as you do so, your awareness gets so used to moving into a mediumistically sensitive state after you speak your opening that the opening moves you into the power easily. You may already begin to pick up on a presence before you even get to the end! Make sure you still complete the opener because it is more for your sitter than it is for you.

Moving Into the Power

Either during the opening spiel or during the time period where you are quiet, you will start to feel the atmosphere and your awareness begin to change around you. This is the power. You may begin to feel dissociated from the moment a bit as well as a pressure at the back of your neck, a thickening of the atmosphere, a sense of lightheadedness or heat. It will feel slightly different for everyone, but it marks that the spirit world is beginning to draw near. Remember, the power precedes phenomena—in this case, the phenomena is mental mediumship.

Making a Link

As soon as you begin to feel the power, you should assume that a presence is nearing you. Take note of the atmosphere around you. Do you sense a presence? You can usually sense a thickening of the atmosphere either on one side of your body or perhaps in front or behind you. Wherever you feel this thickening, gently relax and open your awareness in that general direction. You may then begin to feel a centralized sense of pressure, thickness, or density. This is where your spirit communicator is.

You can begin to describe this to your sitter. "I am beginning to feel the pressure of a presence building up in the atmosphere to my _____" (_____ being whatever direction you are experiencing the presence). As you say this, the energy should begin to change. This is where our practice of "notice, accept, and let it go" from sitting in the power begins to play out. Instead of "notice, accept, and let it go," we now "notice, *express*, and let it go." We notice the change in the energy, we describe it to our sitter, and then we let it go to make room for the next impression that is coming in. We repeat this process to create the conveyor belt of information that comes to us from the spirit world.

I often refer to this process as "pulling the thread" of the experience. This is because it may begin as subtle and light, but as we describe and continue to "pull the thread" by describing our experience and then letting the next thing come, the link becomes much more obvious, detailed, and stronger.

The Triangle of Communication

When we are connecting with a spirit communicator, there are three components that must be functioning well to establish a clear link with the spirit world. The medium, the sitter, and the spirit communicator must all be working together in concert to have the strongest result. You can think of this as a triangle of energetic connection, or as I often explain it to my students, a wheel of water that we must keep spinning to maintain the communication.

The first component of the three is the spirit communicator. The spirit communicator must want to connect with the sitter and begin to impress themselves onto the medium. This is the initial passing of the energy to the medium. This will be experienced by the power changing in the atmosphere around the medium. Through this change, the medium knows that there is someone who wishes to communicate with the sitter.

The next component is the medium. As the medium becomes sensitive, they begin to sense the presence of the spirit communicator. It is the power of the medium, which they have cultivated over time, that is used to establish the link. As the medium opens their energy, they are able to sense and feel where the spirit is around them. The medium receives the energy passed to them from the spirit world. They will then begin to describe whatever is impressed upon them. This is the next passing of the energy, now onto the sitter.

The third component of a communication is the sitter. As the sitter receives the description from the medium about who they are sensing, the sitter then acknowledges and validates the information. The act of validating and recognizing the information the medium is describing then sends energy back to the spirit communicator and completes the circle of the flow of energy to start again. Each time the sitter acknowledges the correct information, it empowers the spirit communicator even more and intensifies the energy and the strength of the link. The medium is then able to receive even more accurate information, which the sitter validates again, and the link is further strengthened. This continues throughout the duration of the reading, and hopefully each pass increases the power and the accuracy of the reading.

Once you have made the link to the spirit communicator, you will want to let go of any specific direction that it needs to go. Just continue to describe your experience and let yourself be led by the spirit. Let them bring to you what they want to talk about. Avoid trying to ask questions of the spirit. Open-ended questions are okay, such as "What else would you like to give?" or simply "What else?" Avoid direct questions to the spirit communicator earlier on in your development as asking direct questions will often be answered by your mind. For example, asking "What is your name?" will almost always lead to your mind answering the question for you. If the spirit wants to bring you their name, they will. Hand over the communication to the other world and just report on the experience; don't interpret it.

In general, I train my students to just follow spirit's lead. Believe it or not, I almost never ask direct questions of the spirit communicator when I do a reading. This is because I have developed such trust in my mediumship that I know the spirit will bring me whatever is needed for the sitter. Open-ended questions are okay, such as "What else would you like to give?" or "Is there anything else you want to say about that?" The mind is not as likely to try to answer the question if the question is open-ended.

That being said, this does not mean we can never ask questions of the spirit. You absolutely can and the spirit will answer it. The key is that you must have already cultivated the ability to stay neutral regardless of whatever is being asked of you. If you can maintain an indifference to the outcome and not try to look for the answer, it will usually come.

In general, if you can develop to simply follow the lead of the spirit communicator, you will rarely, if ever, need to ask a question of the spirit. Often in my readings, if a sitter comes with a list of questions, the spirit will answer the questions point by point, in order! Other times they can describe details that I never would have thought to ask about, such as the time the spirit communicator reviewed her last will and testament point by point and asked when her ashes were going to be turned into memorial diamonds and distributed to her grandchildren. This was all validated by the sitter. It is amazing what kinds of information the spirit world can bring when you leave it in their capable and intelligent hands.

Reading Tips

Now that you have the link up and running, here are some reading tips to keep the link flowing and going smoothly.

Take It Moment to Moment

Just take the experience moment to moment. Don't try to rush it or force it. Far too often, students feel like there is a speed at which they should be reading. They will often want to make the flow of the information come quicker. This will come with time. For now, just notice what you are experiencing moment to moment. It is better to get a slow yes than a fast no. Learn to lean in to the communicator rather than try to fill in the gaps because nothing new is coming. It will come if you notice what you're aware of, describe it, and then fully let it go.

Put Aside Desire, Distraction, and Expectation

As discussed in chapter 6, remember to set aside desire for an outcome, distraction of your own thoughts and your sitter's reactions, and your expectations on how the reading should look, feel, or flow. Each one of these experiences creates tension. Mediumship works the best when we are free from tension and trusting ourselves and our experiences. Do not worry about getting specific types of information or trying to get specifics. Just deliver whatever is coming to you. If you can feel yourself reaching, just allow yourself to relax back into your heart space and feel out into the atmosphere until you can feel the sensations again. Take it one step at a time.

Intend It, Don't Will It

As mentioned before, there is a difference between willing something to happen versus intending something to happen. Think of will as a fist and intent as an open hand. When we will something to happen, we are making it happen. We are actively deciding that something will come out of our own desire and direction. Intent, on the other hand, is much lighter, less intense or deliberate. Intent holds the possibility of something without forcing it into being. In mediumship we want to intend a connection with our spirit communicator; we do not will it. We want to be open to the possibility, which can be one of many. It is keeping an open palm to the spirit world and saying, "I wait for you to take my hand." If you find that you are forcing any part of the reading, take a step back and remember to patiently wait for the experience to happen to you, not originate from you.

Describe, Don't Interpret

This is the most common mistake I see students and even professional mediums make. They will interpret what their experience is rather than just describe it. When the spirit world impresses us with an experience, we should be delivering it exactly as we are experiencing it. Do not try to come to a conclusion as to what they are trying to say. In mediumship the information is not normally symbolic. Mediumship is more about describing what is happening in the moment and letting each new part of the experience add layers to what you are describing.

A great example of the value of describing versus interpreting the information coming to you came when I was working with a lady who had lost her son. After giving great detail as to who her son was, how he had passed, and other identifying evidence, I handed the reading over to the spirit communicator and let him talk about whatever he wanted. I was then impressed that he wanted to speak about a letter that was written for him by his mother. She validated that she had written a letter about him. I could feel myself wanting to reach for more information about this letter, so I backed off and relaxed more into what I was feeling. I began to feel a pressure on my head.

Now here is where I could have gone wrong and begun to interpret the experience. A pressure on the head can mean so many different things—a head injury, a hat, depression, mental confusion—there are so many options. I let the next piece of information come and felt that he was making reference to a hat. Again, instead of interpreting, I just

Chapter 11

described, "Your son is making me aware of a type of hat that is important." I let the next impression come. He gave me an image of a bike, so I
said, "And now he is showing me a picture of a bike."

The mother exclaimed, "Yes! The letter was about a bicycle helmet!"
At any point had I interpreted or tried to make sense of the chunks of
information coming to me, I may have misinterpreted what the son was
trying to say to me. The letter could have been about anything, and yet
he gave me exactly what the letter was about: a very special bicycle helmet he had as a child. Just deliver your information exactly as it is happening, even if it makes no sense to you.

Oftentimes when a sitter gives you a no to a piece of information that
you have given them, it is more often the interpretation that is wrong
rather than the stimulus that made you want to say what you said.
Should you get a no in a message, check in with yourself: "Did I say that
exactly how I experienced it? What did I experience exactly that made
me say what I said? What was the actual stimulus?" Then give what the
stimulus was. When I have made this correction with students during
their reading, nine out of ten times, the sitter could take the information
when the actual stimulus was described rather than the interpretation.
Just narrate your experience and trust what you are feeling. This will save
you a lot of challenges.

Follow the Yeses

When you are giving a reading, notice how you receive the information.
If you are giving lots of feelings and you get yeses when you describe
your feelings, trust that. If you are giving lots of pictures and your sitter can take those, keep giving the pictures. However, if every time
you give a picture you saw in your mind, your sitter says no to it, stop
using your pictures and trust your feelings. This is true for any one of
the clairs. Follow the way the information is coming that is correct and
ignore the way the information is coming to you that is leading you to
incorrect information.

EXERCISE

Experience Connecting with a Spirit Communicator

This exercise works best with a partner. Have your partner only respond with *yes* if they can understand the information, *no* if they cannot, *I don't know* if they are unsure, or *I need more information* if they aren't sure yet. To be clear, an *I don't know* is not a *no*. Remember that once you can feel the presence with you, you are describing a person, so the experiences you have should be descriptive of who this person is rather than just random thoughts and images.

Begin by attuning your awareness to the spirit world. When you can begin to feel the sensations that let you know you are attuned, i.e., tingling, buzzing, pressure in the atmosphere around you, you can move to the next step. Offer the intent "Who would like to come forward for my partner?" and then immediately return to your relaxed and neutral state. Do not start looking for any information; just allow yourself to remain neutral and passive. You are waiting for a change in the atmosphere.

As soon as you feel something beginning to shift, start describing the energetic changes that are occurring. Perhaps you feel a pressure building up on one side specifically or even a tingling or breeze focused in a particular area. Give voice to these sensations. If they begin to increase as you speak about them, there is likely a spirit communicator with you.

Try to stay relaxed and do not get too excited. Just notice the experience, describe it, and then let it go. Allow yourself to continue to do this and let yourself be inspired by whatever arises.

Ideally, always include what you're feeling even if you give pictures. Whatever you experience, deliver this to your partner. "I am aware of [whatever you are experiencing]." Follow that with, "And as I relax into that, I begin to become aware of…" and describe whatever you are experiencing by the time you reach the end of the sentence. Give whatever is coming.

Once you have given one piece of information, let yourself go right back to what you are experiencing. Be sure to elicit a response from your sitter after each new idea or concept: "Does this make sense to you?" Notice the power and the energy around you. When you give accurate information, how does the atmosphere change? Allow yourself to follow this process as long as you can. If you get three no's in a row, you can stop or try to see if there is another communicator.

When you feel that no more information is coming or the power is dropping, you can thank the spirit for coming forward and return to normal awareness.

12

Learning to Recognize Spirit People by Their Essence

In the last chapter, we began to make a link with the spirit communicator and begin to describe our experience as it changed. In this chapter, we will be learning how to deepen our understanding of the essence of the spirit communicator.

No matter who you meet in your day-to-day life, you get a sense of who they are. Whether it is the stranger on the street, your mother, your best friend, or your crazy aunt, there is a feeling sense we all experience that gives us information about how that person makes us feel. We use this sense to tell us information about who someone is. For example, imagine that through the front door walks in a rugged man's man who loves hunting, fishing, and whittling wood. He is a strong, sturdy man that doesn't express too many emotions on the outside but is a silent feeler. You may already begin to be feeling an emotion or an energy that you associate with this kind of personality. Now, instead, imagine that in the front door walks a small white-haired grandmother type who smells of perfume and is gentle, sweet, and caring. Notice how these two examples instill a different reaction internally for you. Where do you experience them within your being?

For most people, this feeling sense will arise somewhere between the heart space and the solar plexus. This is our feeling region. To illustrate this, imagine that you are walking down a street at night. You see a man walking toward you on the same side of the street with a hoodie on, ripped jeans, a bit disheveled, not menacing but not smiling. Where within you do you feel a response? It doesn't matter who they are or how they act; we will have an automatic sense of who someone is as we sense them in our space. This sense of them gets even clearer and more nuanced as we get to know them and get a better understanding of who they are.

EXERCISE
Sensing Physical Essence

By focusing on this feeling sense that arises within you, we are beginning to understand people by their essence first. An excellent way to begin to strengthen this is with the help of a couple of friends. One person will act as the medium, and they will be placed in a chair facing away from the other two individuals. Then, before beginning the exercise, have the first friend step up right behind the medium and say their name. This friend should stand there for a few moments so that the medium can get a sense of their essence—how they energetically feel as they step into their energy. Then have the first friend step back. The second friend can come forward and repeat the steps that the first friend did by saying their name and standing behind the medium for a few moments. Once the medium has a good sense of how each feels, the exercise can begin.

Have the medium, who is still facing away from the two friends, begin to feel the atmosphere around them and become sensitive to the energetic space in their aura. Now, without telling the medium who is stepping forward, have one of the two friends stand behind the medium. The medium should then say which friend they believe it to be. Then have them step back.

Next, either the same person or the second friend may step behind the medium. Have the medium say who they feel it is. The goal is to have the medium accurately say who is standing behind them just by feeling the essence of their friends. You can continue this several times and then, at the end, tell the medium how many they got correct.

For this exercise to work well, be mindful of your smell, footsteps, and breathing noises you make. You want the physical experience to be as neutral for your medium as possible to avoid accidentally using other cues to determine who is stepping forward. If your medium begins to become quite good at this, you can move to ear plugs and multiple friends. This will increase the challenge of the experience.

People Are Complex

People are multifaceted and layered. So while we may have a certain feeling about the random person we see on the street, this is a very different sense that we have when we get to know them. Think of a friend that when you first met them, you either didn't like them or found some kind of fault in them initially. Then, as you got to know them, you saw them in a more complete picture and it changed your perspective of them greatly. This is the same concept. Through our relationship with someone, we begin to understand them differently. In this example, we see two things showing up about how we interpret someone's essence. One is the way that we feel upon initially meeting someone, and the second is how our relationship to them changes how we understand or feel about them. It will be important for you to understand these two ideas as we continue in the chapter because it highlights the multilayered quality of people. When we first interact with a spirit person for the first time, we might get an initial sense of who that person is; however, when we dig a little deeper, we get beyond the first initial layer that presents itself to us.

While it is easy to want to put people in clear boxes to understand them easily, it is important for us to recognize we cannot say someone is just one way. Often we want to place people into predetermined ideas of who someone is to better understand them. These are archetypes. Archetypes are universal patterns of behaviors or personalities that we identify with to help us understand people. It is common for us to put archetypes to people's personalities to understand who they are. When it comes to mediumship, we need to avoid this. While there will be aspects of a person that fit a given archetypal personality type, people are complex and layered. For example, you can have a lady presenting as an archetypal sweet grandmother who loves cooking, knitting, and taking care of the home. We don't want to then extrapolate that she also must have loved baking cookies with the kids, that she was emotionally present for and available to the grandkids or family, and that she never cheated on her husband. While this may be true of her, we don't want to then make assumptions as to other parts of her personality or lived experiences.

Letting the spirit communicator be multilayered and multifaceted is one of the biggest challenges mediums will face in the beginning of their journeys. This is because they have not fully mastered the ability to tell what is coming from their minds versus what is coming from the spirit world. The medium's mind is then able to slip some of this archetypal thinking into the communication and end up giving incorrect information about the spirit communicator. The best way to avoid this is by describing what you are getting as it is happening without interpretation. By doing this, we will avoid letting our thinking mind change the information coming through. This is often when I tell my students to "stop listening to your reading." What I mean is don't let the information that you are bringing through color where you think the information must lead to next. If we continue to allow each impression that comes from the spirit world to come to us, stimulus by stimulus, we can avoid our minds and focus, instead leaving our connection to the communicator and maintaining an open and neutral perspective.

This next exercise will help you learn how to truly identify how we feel into the essence of the spirit communicator by first practicing how we feel into the essence of those we already know who are living.

EXERCISE

Discovering Where and How You Feel the Essence

The essence exercise is used to help us identify two things: (1) where we feel the essence of the communicator within our being, and (2) how we move through the layers of a personality and a relationship connection. We will be using our imagination to pretend that this friend or family member is walking into the room and sitting next to you—not just as a mental thought but truly imagining them there next to you. Their smell, the space that they take up, their breathing, their voice—really make them living and breathing right there next to you. This is essential for this exercise. Then, when they come into the space, what is the first thing that changes within you? How do you feel differently? Is it a happy feeling or a sense of tension or dread? And where did you feel this within your being? Notice that space as you move through each layer. You will describe each feeling that arises layer by layer.

Avoid mental analysis of the individual. People tend to start out by feeling the presence of their family or friend but will then start to mentally describe this. Be very aware of what the individual layer and stimulus feels like each time. It may be helpful when you do this exercise to place your hand on your heart.

Step one is to describe the personality or essence of this person. Not what you mentally already know, but how you are affected by their presence when they walk into the room. A great way to keep the correct focus is to ask yourself, "How would I feel in this person's presence if I just met them? What is the first thing I would notice?" Then you speak that. Then notice what arises behind that. Is there an emotion or a feeling that replaces this? This is a free association so whatever arises in the moment is what you will describe. If done correctly, you may do this exercise on more than one occasion using the same person and have different answers. This is because you are describing what arises within you *in the moment*, not what you think. Think of these as layers. Each single stimulus is one layer. Deliver that, then let the next thing come. This will be the second layer, and so on.

The second step is to describe how the relationship feels between you and this person. If you could imagine a cord between the two of you, how does it feel? What does it look like? What arises within you about the dynamic of the relationship? Again, avoid thinking about this. As this person is in the space next to you, what is the single stimulus/feeling that comes up for you? Once you have delivered that layer, allow yourself to experience the next layer. What is the next thing inspired within you in the moment?

Here is an example of how this exercise should look:

The person I am using is my best friend. I am imagining that he is in the space next to me. I can feel him there.

The very first layer I feel is a warmth in my heart that feels like love. As I relax into that, the next layer I feel is excitement and joy of being in his presence.

Now that I am connected to the emotion of my friend's presence, I will ask myself, "How would I feel if I had just met him?"

The first layer that arises within me is a warm presence and friendliness. As I relax into that, the next layer that arises is talkative and playful. As I relax into that, the next layer that arises is a sense of gregariousness and good sense of humor.

As I relax into that, I begin to feel a sense of depth to him—someone who thinks about life deeply. As I relax into that, I can feel a desire to be accepted and loved by those around him. As I relax into that, I feel someone who wants to do right by everyone in all situations—a sense of fairness being important. As I relax into that, I can feel that family is important to him.

Notice that as I was feeling into him, I started to describe a little more detail about him because that was what was arising within me in that moment. You can continue on as long as you can go or until you feel you've sufficiently described this person.

Next you will describe the relationship between you and this person.

As I begin to feel into this relationship, it feels like a very deep and strong bond. As I relax into that, I can feel a great depth of love for him. As I relax into that, I can feel a sense of evenness in our support of one another, as if each of us is equally present for the other. As I relax into that, I can feel a time-tested feeling—the feeling that we have been through many ups and downs of life together.

And you can keep going as long as you can feel more. While this relationship happened to be positive, know that this exercise can be done with more challenging relationships as well. I would encourage you to include at least one when you do this exercise. Each time you relax into the experience, you are noticing a new layer of whatever arises in the moment. In this way, we are practicing to notice where this feeling arises within us as well as how to follow the layers, stimulus by stimulus.

Now it's your turn. You will want to select three or four living friends or relatives to describe. For example, your mom, your best friend, and your sister. Write these relationships or the name of the friend on small pieces of paper. Place these pieces of paper in a hat or a bowl and mix them up. Before selecting one from the bowl, take a moment to feel into your inspiration center within—that space containing your heart and solar plexus. Pull the first name out of the bowl and begin the exercise, describing the personality/essence and then the relationship. When you have finished, pull another name from the bowl and start the exercise again. Notice how the energy changes and how and where the inspiration changes within you. Do note that often with more challenging relationships, we can have a tendency to move into our thinking mind. Avoid this and just notice what arises within and narrate that.

Checking In with Your Feeling Space

Now that you know where you feel this inspiration within you and how to describe the layers that arise along the way, you can apply this to your mediumship. The key comes in that feeling place within—the area between the heart space and the solar plexus. We will call it our "feeling space" or "inspiration space." As we learned in previous chapters how to sense the presence of a communicator and then describe what is changing in our experience, here we take it to the next level. Now we are not just describing our sensations but also checking in with this inspiration space. As we feel the communicator stepping into our energy, we will describe the sensations that they bring, but now that we know how to check into that inspiration space within us, we will keep our awareness open to what we notice in this space as well.

Just like we did with the essence exercise with living people, we will notice how this spirit person inspires us within. How would we feel if we met them for the first time? This provides us with evidence of essence. Then we move to the way the relationship feels between the communicator and the sitter. What is inspired within you? How do you change? What sensations change? Do you get a sense of love, guilt, remorse, excitement? Describe these changes. By using what is inspired within us, we are utilizing the whole of the clairsentient experience—the sensations and the inspirational impression from within.

Through this journey of describing the communicator's essence and then relationship, we start to be able to uncover the story of the spirit communicator. Be open to the experience taking you on the life journey of the spirit communicator—the highs and the lows. Let the spirit communicator lead the experience while you just describe what changes from moment to moment. Try not to overthink it or even understand what is coming through; just narrate. Leave the understanding to the sitter. In time, you may come to understand quickly what the spirit communicator is trying to convey; however, it is not a requirement. Just describe what's occurring and follow the flow. The rest will take care of itself.

13

Discerning and Delivering Quality Evidence

In the previous chapter, we explored how to take our sensations and turn them into usable inspiration. Through beginning to describe our communicator in how they inspire and impress us, we are able to begin describing who our spirit communicator is. This is the beginning of the evidence portion of a spirit communication.

Evidence is the information we deliver to our sitter that helps them identify who is communicating from the spirit world. It also allows our sitter to be certain that who the medium says is communicating truly is. By providing an abundance of information about the spirit communicator's personality, relationship to the sitter, and lived experiences, we are able to paint the spirit communicator back to life for our sitter. The sitter should then be able to validate and verify the information as it comes through. This is essential for quality mediumship. A sitter should never accept a message from someone in spirit if they do not know who it's coming from.

Evidence is the cornerstone of quality mediumship. As we learned in the history of mediumship, evidence is what demonstrates that the spirit world is real and can be experienced in real and tangible ways. Through evidence we rule out that the information coming to us comes from normal means—that there truly is a spirit communicator who inspires us and shows us they continue on. This is how we, as mediums, prove survival of consciousness beyond bodily death. Evidence also provides our sitter with information that will pinpoint who is communicating, which is necessary so that any message the spirit person brings can be accepted. We would not want to accept any message that is brought to us unless evidence is presented because otherwise anyone could say anything to you and say it is coming from a loved one in spirit. There is no proof that this individual has any real connection to the spirit world. Evidence provides proof, which is what makes mediumship valuable and is the reason a person visits with a medium. While no one can prove survival to everyone, by providing quality evidence of many sorts, each sitter will find the evidence that is valuable and meaningful to them. Therefore, understanding what constitutes quality evidence is important for the developing medium.

The quality of evidence, in part, is what determines the quality of the mediumship reading. The more accurate and specific the medium can be about the life and relationship of the spirit communicator, the better the reading and the more the message that comes after the evidence can be trusted. So what constitutes quality evidence? Quality evidence can take many forms, but the overall concept is clear, factual, identifying information that can be validated by the sitter.

Types of Evidential Information

For the sake of clarity, I divide these into two types of evidential information: list information and personal evidence. Together they make up a fuller, more accurate and meaningful picture of the spirit communicator.

List Information

I use the term "list" to describe this kind of evidence because it is the type of information that could be read off of a list of facts about a person.

Examples of list information can include:

» names

» age

» relationship to sitter (mother, brother, cousin, friend)

» birthdays or anniversaries

» physical descriptions of the communicator

» how and when they passed to the spirit (accident, cancer, brain aneurysm, etc.)

» familial structure (Were they married? Did they have children? Pets?)

» educational background

» work or career

» location specific information (country, state, city of origin)

» street names or addresses

» specific accomplishments in their life (won a Nobel peace prize, graduated magna cum laude, was a sergeant in the army)

This is not an exhaustive list but an example of the kinds of information that can be received and essentially could be read off of a fact sheet about a loved one in spirit. This kind of evidence is important to get because it helps identify easily who the communicator is. Our job as mediums is to paint as clear of a picture for our sitter as possible. List information provides cut-and-dried facts that can either be accepted by the sitter or not. There is no interpretation with this kind of information; it is or is not true. When added together, list information can be incredibly evidential and validating because this information is coming to the medium by no normal means of attainment. It is coming from the spirit communicator, which can be a very compelling argument for suggesting the survival of consciousness.

List information is important; however, it is not the full picture in providing evidence. The problem with list information alone is that skeptics can argue that this evidence is essentially researchable. These kinds of facts can often be found in any kind of research on a person; therefore, it is important for a medium to also provide another type of evidence: personal evidence.

Personal Evidence

I use the term "personal" for this form of evidence because it is evidence that could only be known if someone knew the spirit communicator personally. This kind of evidence is excellent at helping the sitter recognize the communicator in ways that were important and meaningful to them in their life. By providing this kind of information in addition to list information, we can truly paint the communicator back to life in both a factual way as well as a personal way.

Personal evidence includes:

- » personality (essence of the communicator—how you would feel if you had met them)

- » the quality of the relationship between the sitter and the communicator (they were very close to you, it was a rocky relationship, you were two peas in a pod)

- » shared memories (holidays, special or important vacations, final moments of the spirit communicator's life)

- » nicknames or terms of endearment

- » relationship dynamics amongst family or friends

- » personal challenges faced by the spirit communicator

- » passions or interests (poet, mountain biker, knitter, equestrian)

- » code words (agreed-upon phrases or words to bring forward if they were able to communicate after crossing to the spirit world)

- » other loved ones in spirit whom they have met up with

» spirit-validating paranormal experiences such as dreams, visitations, and signs

» relationship to faith

» personal idiosyncrasies or habits (jingled coins in pocket, whistled all the time, always carried a pen and a pad of paper)

» scents associated with the spirit communicator

» meaningful music or songs

While this is not an exhaustive list of what counts as personal evidence, it is a great starting point. As you can see, personal evidence colors in the essence and lived experience of the spirit communicator's life. It can add a great deal of detail that only the sitter would know, and it truly personalizes the communication, which can sometimes feel sterile when it is just facts and figures. When a sitter comes to you for a reading, they are often seeking this kind of evidence because it is largely connected with the heart of how we remember someone. As the saying goes, "People may not remember what you said, but they will always remember how you made them feel."

What Quality Evidence Is Not

Now that you know what quality evidence can be, let us explore what is not considered quality evidence.

Information That Can't Be Validated

In general, information that is not considered evidential is that which cannot be validated by the sitter. This does not automatically mean that if something cannot be validated by the sitter, it is not good evidence. In fact, there are plenty of times that information must be looked up or asked of someone else that is not known to the sitter at the time and is later validated. As mentioned in chapter 1, this is called research evidence and is an excellent form of evidence in that it excludes the possibility of mind reading, as some may suggest is occurring.

The kind of information that I am clarifying here as not quality evidence is information that can never be validated by the sitter. This can include information about chakras, ascended masters, aliens, or otherworldly creatures. This kind of information is excluded from evidential readings because they cannot be proved in any way. I can say that you have an ascended master working with you, but unless you have some kind of proof of this, the sitter cannot accept this. In general, most energetic descriptions of the sitter's energy should not be considered evidential mediumship, so talking about things like blocked chakras or needing to ground in nature is not evidential.

Psychic Information

Another type of information that may arise in a reading that is not considered evidential mediumship is psychic information. The truth is, psychism can slip into your mediumship readings at times. Often this occurs when the medium is feeling disconnected or perhaps feels tension and then may start to read the energy of the sitter rather than the spirit. Knowing when you are getting information from the spirit versus information from the energy of your sitter is something a developing medium must learn to discern between. Remember, the difference between a psychic and a mediumship reading is the source from where the medium is receiving the information. If the information is coming from the energy of the sitter, it is psychic. If the information is coming from the presence of the spirit communicator, then it is mediumistic.

In theory, one could give a psychic reading that can feel like a mediumship reading because a good psychic can move into the energy of the sitter and discuss the way a passed loved one is remembered within the sitter's energy. This, however, is a very different experience from feeling the presence of a loved one during a mediumship reading. First, in an actual mediumship reading, there is a sense of the power present. Second, we also feel the physical pressure or presence of a spirit communicator through the thickening or pressurizing of the atmosphere around you. There are other clairsentient sensations that occur, such as tingles, chills, and breezes, which indicate a spirit presence is working with you. The information should be coming from the space where you are experiencing this presence. Psychic readings, while they can be very evidential, are not evidential mediumship, and therefore do not count as quality evidence. A developed medium needs to be able to just do a psychic reading or just do a mediumship reading when requested.

Fear-Based, Predictive, or Interfering Information

It is also important for a medium to recognize when their mind is coming into the reading. This is often evidenced by the type of information coming through. For example, the spirit world will never give information that is negative or that creates fear. If they ever do bring forward something that is upsetting, they will almost certainly give a solution or present it in such a way that it is empowering rather than disempowering. I have never had a negative proclamation brought through by the spirit that wasn't also an invitation on how to avoid or get past the situation. Generally, mediumistic information is not predictive. I do not believe that our spirit loved ones can see what is going to happen, and if they can, that view is limited. So I would be hesitant to accept as evidence any kind of predictive information that is well into the future.

The spirit world is generally not going to bring forward information about death, disease, divorce, or disaster, or the four D's. While this information may be attained through a psychic awareness, the spirit world will not bring information like this to the sitter as they do not wish to cause anxiety and stress for us in our lives. Making predictions of a devastating nature will almost always be coming from the mind of the medium, not from the spirit world. It is therefore important for the medium to be aware when this kind of information may start to seep in. It is most likely the mind coming in. Related to this, a spirit communicator will never dictate what needs to happen in a sitter's life. There is no dictating the life of the sitter by the spirit communicator or the medium. All that the spirit person can give is their perspective, just as they might do in life. It is not an edict or a requirement for the sitter to follow this information. In all my years of experience with giving messages, I have never received a genuine message from the spirit world that was telling my sitter "you MUST do this." They are not mad at you or holding grudges against you. Those in the world of spirit recognize that this life is a play, that life is continuous, and that we are here to learn and grow. They do not need to interfere with that process.

Information That's Lacking Context

Lastly, providing random bits of information without any context or further information is not evidential. For example, if I were to become aware of a book, I could not just give, "They are showing me a book; does this make sense to you?" This is not enough information to do anything with. Another example would be giving several unrelated things all at once and seeing what fits. I call this "spaghetti" reading. Let's say I were to get a house, a river, and a casket. I couldn't just deliver that to my sitter and expect them to sort it out. When we do this, we are just giving pieces of information that then rely on the sitter to sort it out in their mind. Yes, it is not the medium's job to understand the information, but it is the medium's job to provide as much information as they can. Ideally there should also be some kind of context to the information coming through—something that will give the sitter an ability to understand how it all fits together.

By encouraging quality evidence and disregarding the nonevidential information we may become aware of, we become more accurate and specific in the information we are bringing through. This is essential to quality work within mediumship and will save you a lot of floundering and confusion in your spirit communications.

How to Get Quality Evidence

Now that we know what quality evidence is, we need to know how we actually get it. We have already begun the process of gathering evidence by working with our sensing and feeling up to this point. We have turned random sensations into descriptors for personality and essence. Now we take it to the next level by learning how to flow with a spirit communication and the power.

Feeling Essence First

First and foremost, you will be much more successful if you learn to understand the power and the flow of a communication. Rather than viewing it at the outset that "I need to get this or that kind of information," we want to come to the communication without any kind of attachment to the outcome and with a mindset of surrender, learning to just describe what we are experiencing as it is happening. It is no good trying to interpret or understand the information. Instead, at the beginning of your development, we want to just narrate what our experience is. So just as we have been doing in previous chapters, as we move into the evidence, we want to follow along what our experience is.

In general, we construct the evidence in such a way that creates an easy-to-follow explanation of who the spirit communicator is. I often recommend that my students begin with the essence of the communicator. As we have been working on the feeling and sensing of the presence, this is the most obvious way to begin.

By describing how our experience of our energy and the presence of the communicator is changing as they step into our energy, we begin the flow of the communication and take our first steps into the evidence. Especially for newer mediums, I do not recommend beginning with a picture of what the spirit communicator looks like unless you have found your pictures to be very accurate and provide you with consistent yeses whenever you deliver visuals you see. I say this because oftentimes when we start with pictures, it does two things. First, it can create less of a close link with the spirit. When we describe something that we see, there is a sense that this thing is separate from us and we are describing it "over there" rather than having a close and personal feeling experience with the communicator. By starting with the essence, we allow them to step into our energy and draw them very near very quickly. This speeds up the blending process. Second, sometimes when we start with a visual of the spirit communicator, our sitter will only think of the people who have whatever specific characteristics you have assigned to them. For example, you may begin by describing someone and say they have a mustache. As you continue the message, all the other information you have been giving is clear, specific, and accurate, but your sitter then says, "I can't take any of it because the man I'm thinking it sounds like didn't have a mustache." Believe me, this does happen, especially with people who are not familiar with how mediumship works. They get very attached to the physical description and then cannot get past that perhaps the mustache is not very important. This is why I think it is always best to start with the essence. People can very easily recognize someone's essence.

Describing the Changes as They Happen

Start by describing what is changing in the atmosphere around you, even if at first you are just describing the energy. "I feel a sense of calm and relaxation. As I relax into the energy, I start to notice _____" (whatever it is that changes or you notice when you reach the end of that sentence). As you describe that next piece of information, allow yourself to describe again what changes. "I begin to feel a thickening of the atmosphere around me, particularly on my right side." Assume, as we have learned from the previous chapters, that this is a communicator stepping forward. As you feel this presence, how do you begin to change? What do you begin to feel? Describe the essence of the communicator. "This feels like a man who would have been quite warm and inviting. As I relax into his presence, I begin to feel that he is older than me and feels older than the sitter. This feels like he would be a generation above you." You should give at least three to five pieces of information prior to checking in with your sitter for the first time. "I feel that this is a male, he feels quite warm and inviting, he feels like he's older than you, I feel a fatherly sense with him, he makes me feel like he loved golfing, and he use to drive a truck." Once you have given your three to five pieces of information, you can then ask if this makes sense to your sitter. Assuming that they validate your information, you can then give the next bit of information.

Now, as you move forward with the communication, after each new idea or concept, you should check in with your sitter to make sure that makes sense to them. "I know that your father enjoyed gambling and would visit the casino regularly. Does this make sense to you?" You would not want to say, "I know your father enjoyed gambling and would visit the casino regularly. He would also go diving in the ocean off of a boat called 'Shenanigans.' He also was married for fourteen years and owned six dogs in his lifetime." Notice how in the second example, multiple pieces of unrelated information were given without checking after each new concept. This can lead to confusion for your sitter because they may be able to take some of the information and not all of it. For example, they may be able to take that he enjoyed gambling and was married for fourteen years but could not take the rest of the information. They would not be able to correct you because you have requested they only answer *yes, no, I don't know,* or *I need more information.* Now there is an issue in how they can respond, and it complicates things. Therefore, it is better to just check in after each new idea or concept.

Deliver whatever is coming to you as you feel this presence step in. Each time you give information, keep your attention on the spirit communicator. Do not break your focus from the communicator to get a response from your sitter. You can elicit a response from your sitter while simultaneously keeping your attention on your spirit communicator. As they give you their voice, notice how the power changes. When you give correct information or you are validated by your sitter, the sense of the spirit communicator should increase. When you feel this increase, notice, accept it, and relax more into it. This is usually when they are bringing you more information. The more you are relaxed and free of tension, the clearer the communication will be. The power will tell you how the communication is going. The stronger or more intense you can feel it, the more you know you are staying in the flow. Should you feel it start to dissipate, you will know that your mind or tension is coming into your reading. To fix this, just begin to relax back into the communication and surrender more. It also helps sometimes to focus on your heart or solar plexus and get your attention back into what you are feeling rather than focusing on what you are thinking.

As you are moving through the communication, remember that it comes to you piece by piece. I call this the "conveyor belt of communication." Each time you receive a piece of information, you want to notice it, describe it, and then let it go and immediately be ready for the next piece of information or impression that comes to you. There is an assumed sense that more information will arrive as you give the next bit of information. As you give this information, notice what you are drawn to. As you deliver each piece, did you feel a little nudge or subtle pull to a particular thing that you said? This is generally an indication that there is more information there available for you. Allow yourself to flow in that direction with your awareness with a sense of curiosity. What else is there?

Exploring Layers of the Communication

Remember that a spirit communication is all about layers. We often move from broad to more specific if the information doesn't already start out as very specific. For example, I may get an awareness of a baseball. As I experience this, I say to my sitter, "Your father is making me aware of a baseball." Then, as I say that, I notice I begin to be impressed with a great sense of love and happiness around the sport.

"He makes me feel that he had a great love and interest in the sport. It made him very happy." The sitter validates this and as they do, you feel that he actually played the sport. "He makes me feel that he played baseball"—as you say this, you feel when he was younger, around eighteen—"around the age of eighteen." The sitter validates this. You are then impressed with a sense that he did this well into his adult life and was professional. "Your father makes me aware that he played for a long time and was even professional." Your sitter validates this. You then get a sense that he played for a specific team. "He played for the Angels." Your sitter validates this. In this example, notice how the information began with something simple and unspecific, but through allowing the flow of information to arise as you spoke about it, it got progressively more detailed and more specific. You went from a picture of a baseball to played professionally for the Angels.

This is the journey we take when we describe exactly what we are getting rather than try to interpret the information. Take the previous example. I could have easily got baseball and then said, "Your father loved watching baseball on TV" or "Your father loved sports." While that may be true, I may not have gotten the more specific detail that came from just delivering it as it arose. Moreover, seeing a baseball can mean anything from liking sports in general to liking to play baseball to watching baseball to actually hating baseball. It all depends on the context that arises through our clairsentient feeling of the experience as well as the other pieces of information that follow the first piece. Do your best to not try to make a whole message out of one piece of information, i.e., just the baseball. Let yourself uncover and discover what information is there for you as you move along.

Now that we know how to get the information, it is important that we know how to deliver the information. Oftentimes when we get a no in a reading, it has less to do with our information being inaccurate and more to do with our delivery. It is generally how we describe what we are experiencing that creates confusion or lack of clarity.

When we are working with our sitter, it is important for us to get them to give us their voice by responding to the statements regarding the information that we are receiving. We want to elicit a response from our sitter because the vibration of their voice helps strengthen our link with the spirit communicator. We only want our sitter to give us *yes, no, I don't know*, or *I need more information*. By doing this, we are helping eliminate our mind from entering into the reading. As we know more about what is being said, we can tend to want to listen to the reading, and our brain will naturally make associations with what is coming through. By just getting those limited responses, we also reduce the chance of cold reading. Each statement that is given by the medium to the sitter should elicit a response. We do this by either making a statement and asking "Does this make sense to you?" or by phrasing in a way that is making a statement but asking for confirmation: "You would understand that your father worked with his hands." By saying "you would understand," you are asking a question that only requires a yes or a no and does not invite the sitter to give you any further information. You are also still stating the information as fact versus uncertainty. The less information our sitter gives us, the better.

It is also helpful to continuously speak while giving a reading. As you are giving information to the sitter, rather than pausing for a long time until the next bit of information comes, you can add a connective phrase such as "As I relax into this, I become aware of…" This helps you keep the energy flowing by moving the experience along with the words you are saying. It is almost as if you are talking your way into what you're wanting to experience. "As I relax into this" is prompting yourself to let go more so that you are more receptive. "I become aware of" helps you notice what you are becoming aware of in your experience. A simple connective phrase can keep you continuously moving with what is coming rather than getting stuck inwardly.

Another helpful point is to provide the information that is coming to you with a sense of confidence. Rather than saying, "I think I am getting that your father worked with his hands" or "It might mean your father worked with this hands" or "I don't know if this is right, but I think your father worked with his hands," you can say things like, "I know that your father worked with his hands" or "I am being made aware that your father worked with his hands" or "Your father is telling me he worked with his hands." By changing how you phrase a statement into a more confident and certain manner, so too will your connection be stronger for it.

It is important that we learn how to hold space for our sitter as well. While we are working with our sitter, they may begin to feel emotions such as sadness, anger, grief, loss, or hurt. It is important that you, as the medium, are able to hold space for them. By this I mean not trying to end or stop their tears or emotions. This is an important part of the experience. Should they begin to cry, it is helpful to be sensitive, but don't stop the reading because of the tears. Sometimes, if we allow ourselves to pay too much attention to our sitter's emotions, we can make them embarrassed or uncomfortable. It is better to carry on with the reading as this helps the sitter to continue moving through their feelings rather than getting stuck at any one point. It would be less helpful to stop the reading and ask them if they are okay. Just keep moving with it. I have had a sitter specifically thank me at the end of the reading for not letting their emotions stop the reading; by continuing on, it helped them move through that moment.

This is also a great time to mention the emotions of the medium and how we can keep these in check. It is important for us to not get overwhelmed by what we are feeling when we are working with the spirit world. There will be times when you feel very strong and intense emotions, both positive and negative. I have often seen developing mediums become overwhelmed and emotional by the feeling of love between the spirit communicator and the sitter. It is important that we do not let this happen. These are not our emotions; rather, they are what the spirit is trying to communicate to our sitter. Our job is to just deliver the information. If there is an emotion that seems to be very strong and intense, treat it the way you would check if an iron is hot. You just slightly touch the iron very quickly to see if it is warm; you do not hold your hand on the iron or grab it. This would cause a burn. Similarly, you want to touch the strong emotion, notice how it is making you feel, and then deliver that bit of information. It is easy for newer mediums to become overwhelmed by these strong emotions because they are so obvious that it is hard for them to notice anything else. Therefore, we need to always have the intention that as we pass on one part of the information, we are ready for the next impression. The information is always moving, and the next thing will come as soon as we let go of the first. This way, we keep the communication moving and do not get stuck in the strong emotion. The emotion is not ours to feel; it is the spirit's way of sharing and emphasizing what they are feeling. Its purpose is to be passed on exactly how it is experienced. This should cause the emotion to subside.

I am a strong believer that we can say almost anything to anyone in a reading; it is just a matter of how you say it. This can make sensitive topics tricky to navigate. For example, many people have a concern or fear around how to describe a tragic death such as suicide. The medium may become aware of how the sitter passed in detail, but that does not mean that they need to deliver the details of how they passed. The sitter already knows. Instead of saying "Your son died by hanging himself," you can say something much more tactful, such as "Your son tells me he is responsible for his crossing to the spirit world." This is a much more sensitive way to express this. Also, when discussing passing conditions in general, we want to avoid going into great detail as to what happened or how the individual suffered. Oftentimes sitters are very aware of this. Having them relive it in the reading is unnecessary and even unethical. You can speak about the loss of weight in a cancer patient, but you do not have to go into detail: "They were bone-thin." Be considerate of how you speak about those whom your sitter has loved and lost.

Lastly, we do not want to belabor the negative aspects of a person's life. Of course we do not avoid them—those are real parts of the experience of living—but we don't need to make the majority of the reading about harping on a specific detail or issue in someone's life. I often see this with new mediums. They get one theme in someone's life and then continuously refer back to it throughout the reading. "He was a good son, but his depression always made him sad. He loved biking, but his depression often made him lose interest in things. He was a sensitive soul, but he never could kick his addictions and his depression." Don't make your spirit person one-dimensional. They can be many things and have many layers, even contradictory ones. People are often complex. Touch on all parts of someone's life.

EXERCISE

Making a Clear and Evidential Link with a Spirit Communicator

This exercise works best with a partner who will be your sitter.

Your sitter should have a pen and paper and should be writing down each piece of information that you bring through. Alternatively, you could record your reading and review it upon playback. Take note of what was correctly given and what was not. Try to notice how you felt prior to delivering that information—Did any of it feel like you were reaching or coming from your mind? Was there a feeling that came with correct information? This kind of reflection can help you identify how you feel with right information versus wrong information before you even speak it.

You now should have everything you need to make a clear and evidential link. In this exercise we will continue to build on our experiences thus far to receive accurate information from the spirit communicator.

To start, become aware of the atmosphere around you through the process of attunement. Once you have the sensations that let you know you are energetically sensitive, place an intention to connect with a loved one in spirit for your sitter. "Who would like to come forward for my partner?" Immediately return to relaxing and noticing the sensations around you.

We are waiting for a shift in the atmosphere or your awareness.

As you notice a shift, begin to describe what you are feeling. If it is just sensations, that is fine. You should begin to notice a centralized point of sensations such as thickening on one side more than another in the atmosphere or perhaps tingling or temperature change around you in a specific place.

Once you have this, assume it is a communicator and begin to describe what you sense and feel about them. How does their presence change you? This is an excellent place to begin describing the communicator's essence. How would you feel if you had just met them? How does their energy change you? As you receive information, be sure to offer the information in a way your sitter can validate. "You would understand _____ (whatever you are experiencing)." You can say what you are experiencing and say, "Does this make sense to you?" As you get yeses from your partner/sitter, notice the power and how it changes. Once your sitter begins to accept the information, you've already begun to deliver evidence of your communicator.

To take it another step further, allow your spirit communicator to impress you with details about their lives. Becoming curious about who your communicator is can be helpful, but do not ask them a series of questions or your mind may try to answer them.

Just by knowing the possibilities mentioned above, these kinds of information may start to come into your awareness. Describe whatever comes and allow yourself to follow the stimuli moment by moment and see what comes.

When you feel you have given every piece of evidence you can, review it with your sitter and get feedback on what made sense and what did not.

14

Sharing the Message from Loved Ones in Spirit

Evidence is a vitally important aspect to a quality mediumship reading. It lets your sitter know that the spirit stepping forward is who they say they are, which is an essential part of spirit communication. But why do we emphasize the evidence? We emphasize the evidence because it helps our sitter trust the message. In most instances, even more than the evidence, this is why your sitter comes to a medium. They want to hear what their loved ones in spirit have to say to them. They want answers to the things left unsaid, the sorries never given, the forgiveness necessary for them to move past the loss. There are so many loose ends after the passing of someone we love. Many times we do not get to say good-bye or tell someone the last words we wished to have said. For both the spirit communicator and the sitter, this is that moment for them.

Also, the message brings forward evidence of survival in its own right. Oftentimes in a message, spirit communicators will discuss things that have happened since their passing. This not only gives the chance for the spirit to address things they were not here for in life, but they also prove that they are still aware of our lives, that they see what we are doing, and that they still live on beyond the transition of physical death.

The message is such a crucial aspect of spirit communication, but for some reason, it is one of the most neglected portions of development in mediumship. So much emphasis is placed on accurate evidential information to prove the identity and life of the spirit communicator. However, the message should carry just as much weight and importance.

What Constitutes a Message

A message is the portion of the reading where the spirit communicator gets to directly discuss whatever they wish to bring up that is significant and relevant to the sitter and spirit's life or relationship. A message does not need to be saved for the end of the reading. It can be anywhere in the communication, but one should identify who the communicator is first with enough evidential information so the sitter knows exactly who is bringing the message. There would be no value in just providing a message without establishing who the communicator is because our sitter will not know who to attribute it to.

Once the communicator's identity is established, a message can be interspersed between pieces of evidence or it can be at the end of the reading. In the beginning of one's development, it is helpful for learning and training purposes to have a structure of evidence first, and then the message. This will then leave out any potential for spiritless messages. However, once you have developed your mediumship to a sufficient level, be open to the messages appearing at any point in the communication—yes, even at the beginning. Albeit rare, I have given readings where I begin with the emotion or apology from a communicator and then have to give information as to who is communicating. It is not the cleanest approach to the reading because unless it is an incredibly specific message, it can leave your sitter confused as to who this person is for an early part of the reading. They may not take the message to heart if they do not know who it is coming from.

What Is Not a Message

To understand the message more, let us understand what is not the message. The message is not in the evidence. This is a commonly taught technique which states that the message the communicator is wanting to bring is in the evidence about their lives. For example, let us say I was bringing through a sitter's father and he particularly loved nature and being outdoors. This "technique" that the message is in the evidence would often play out as the medium suggesting to the sitter that the message is that your father wants *you* to go out into nature more because it is something that he enjoyed. I cannot express to you how much this kind of message irks me. Firstly, it is lazy mediumship. Secondly, it takes away the opportunity of the spirit communicator to express what *they* wish to say. Lastly, it often leaves the sitter disappointed because of all the things someone's loved one could have come forward to say about their relationship to the sitter, their lives, their thoughts on what's happened since they died, etc., they came forward and said, "I loved nature so you should go into nature." This kind of message will ultimately leave the sitter without what they came for and does not show what is possible in a quality spirit communication.

Another type of message given that does not qualify as a quality message are platitudes. Far too often, developing mediums will offer overused, generalized advice and claim it is coming from the loved one in spirit. For example, a medium gives a series of great evidence—specific, detailed—and then when they come to the message, they say something like, "Live each moment like it's your last, follow your passion, and everything happens for a reason." This kind of message is not coming from the spirit (unless it was a phrase that the loved one used often and is an identifying phrase). More often than not, this message is coming from the mind of the medium because they have not been taught how to properly receive the message portion of a reading. Also, no one goes to a medium to hear generalized advice. They want to hear the words their loved ones want to say to them. There is so much potential for closure, healing, and growth from the message. We should not minimize or generalize it in any way.

Along the lines of platitudes, another type of unhelpful message is overly "spiritual" or "New Agey" advice. This is common among underdeveloped mediums that tend to be in a more ungrounded place in their spiritual development. For example, a male spirit communicator comes forward and is described as rugged, reserved, quiet—a man's man. The medium precedes to give other great evidence that identifies him to the sitter. Then, when they get to the message, the medium unknowingly ditches their communicator and says, "His message is that you need to connect with your divine feminine and that by smoke-cleansing your house you will attract a partner into your life." Obviously this is an exaggeration, but you get the point. Giving "spiritual guidance" as a message from someone who would have never even heard of such a concept makes no sense at all. It takes away from what the communicator would actually like to say and it also is due to the medium's insecurity. Often, when mediums feel insecure around a message or evidence, they will revert to some kind of spiritual advice that they think would apply to the situation. This is usually unconscious. It is why it is so vital that the medium develops awareness of what is coming from their mind versus what is coming from the spirit communicator.

Things That Might Be Included

A message can contain basically anything you can think of. This is because a spirit communicator can address anything from any time of their lives. While certainly not an exhaustive list, below are some examples of what a spirit communicator could impress in a message:

> » Making amends for behaviors while living

> » Making amends for how things were left after their passing

> » Thanking those who supported them during their illness

> » Thanking the sitter for their relationship

> » Personal details about the relationship between the sitter and the spirit communicator

> » Ways that the spirit communicator was remembered (memorials, burials, tattoos) at the time of their passing

» Meaningful words that were spoken to them at the moment of passing

» Current events in the sitter's life

» Congratulations over current or past events since the spirit communicator's passing

» Words of encouragement for current struggles

» Letting their sitter know they are okay

» Sharing their emotions and feelings with the sitter (pride, joy, regret, gratitude)

» Other crossed-over loved ones they have met up with

» Acknowledging pets either living or passed

» Acknowledging children who passed young or never touched the earth

» Giving loved ones permission to move on or date again

While there are no common messages—all are unique—we can see that there are so many more options when it comes to what can come through in a message. This list should serve more as inspiration of what is possible rather than required or limiting in any way. The reality is the spirit world can speak of anything you can possibly imagine, so the more open your mind and your awareness to the possibilities, the more they can share. Also, this list should act more as a starting point rather than a conclusion. Each one of the items listed should have more detail within them through the process of connecting with the communicator.

Examples of Quality Messages

Now that we have discussed what a message is not, what are examples of quality messages? This will all depend on the communicator. Each communicator has their own lives and lived experiences, and it is up to us to do our best to bring forward accurate information that is coming from them. How do we do this? By recognizing that the way we get the evidence from the communicator is the same process we use to get the message from the communicator. What I mean is that it comes in chunks, not necessarily all at once. Just as I explained the idea of a conveyor belt in chapter 13, we get the message the same way—in pieces that can make sense to the sitter. Sometimes we will have an understanding of how they fit together; other times we will not. Remember to deliver the mail, not read it! It is not our job to understand what we are talking about; as long as the sitter understands it, that is what is important.

The message does not have to be some fully formed idea or advice about life. In fact, you may not have an understanding of what the overall point of the message is until the end of the reading because it is forming as you receive each new impression. The message should be applicable to the sitter's life in some way, and often this adds more evidence to the message. For example, I was giving a reading to a lady from her brother. After describing their relationship, details of his passing, and his personality, I relaxed my awareness even further so I might be open to anything he could possibly want to discuss. He began bringing up his wife he left behind. As I felt the next impression, I felt that she was distant and separate from the family. I also felt that there were issues around money and the way things were left. All of this was confirmed by the sitter. As I relaxed more into it, her brother was making me aware that the wife was trying to keep property separate from the sitter's side of the family and that her brother wanted to acknowledge her efforts in trying to right the wrongs done by his ex. He also went on to describe the troubles he had with her, which was again validated by the sitter. He encouraged her to continue the pursuit of acquiring the property and to find the older written will.

Notice how this example of a message has applicable value and evidential elements along the way. The sitter's brother was able to talk about pressing and pertinent issues that were meaningful both to the sitter and to the spirit communicator. He gave his thoughts and his advice on the situation. This had a huge impact on the sitter and gave her validation and confidence that she was doing the right thing—not because I told her or gave her my opinion or a platitude, but because her brother had the chance to discuss what he wanted to discuss. While not all messages will be about current situations, they can still be evidential and important to the sitter.

Say that I was experiencing a feeling of pride for the sitter from the spirit communicator. I would say, "Your father is making me feel proud of you." Most likely, as I noticed the feeling of pride, if I allowed the next impression to be inspired, I would be able to give *why* there is a feeling of pride. Maybe the next layer I felt was relating to school. I would say, "He is making me aware he is proud regarding your school achievement." Assuming the sitter validates this, the next layer may be a feeling of coming to the end of school. I would then offer, "He's making me aware that you are going to be finishing school soon." The sitter validates, and I may then become aware that she is getting a higher level of education, but it also feels like a second degree or level. I would then say, "He's making me aware that you are about to complete your masters program." The sitter validates, and I feel impressed with the date of March 29 and feel this is significant to this situation. "He impresses me that there is a significant event happening on March 29"—as I say this, I get that it is her graduation. "This is when you are graduating, correct?" The sitter validates it is correct. Then I allow her father to add anything else he wants to give. He then impresses that he will be with her when she is receiving her diploma. "He makes me aware that he will be there with you at your ceremony and that he is so excited for you."

Notice how the message unfolded in the above example. It wasn't just packaged all in one hit, but rather through a series of impressions that I was not interpreting but rather relaying exactly how I was experiencing them. Avoid the temptation to understand a small part of the message and then let your mind run away with the rest of the message. Similarly to how we let the information come to us with evidence bit by bit, we do the same here. The detail comes as you go along. Obviously, in the example above, it may not be so segmented. I wanted to illustrate how the chunks could come, but be open that they can come rather rapidly and that you won't necessarily need to check in at each one of these impressions (though there's nothing wrong with checking in then either).

Through the process of allowing the spirit communicator to deliver what they want to talk about, rather than what the medium thinks the message should be, we can truly bring amazing messages to our sitters. Generally, the sitter is there to learn three main things: that their loved one's life still goes on, that they are okay, and what the loved one wants to say to them. It is our job to provide them with the clearest and most authentic message their loved one can give.

EXERCISE
Message-Focused Reading

Now that you have a better understanding of what constitutes a message, let us add it to what we have been doing so far. Remember, a message can come at any point in a reading, but for this exercise, let us put the message at the end. First, we are going to provide evidence of who the communicator is. I want the reading to be 25–50 percent evidence and the rest message. This way we are practicing focusing on the message more than the evidence.

To start, become aware of the atmosphere around you through the process of attunement. Once you have the sensations that let you know you are energetically sensitive, place an intention to connect with a loved one in spirit for your partner/sitter: "Who would like to come forward for my partner?" Immediately return to relaxing and noticing the sensations around you.

We are waiting for a shift in the atmosphere or your awareness. As you begin to notice a shift, begin to describe what you are feeling. If it is just sensations, that is fine.

You should begin to notice a centralized point of sensation such as a thickening on one side more than another in the atmosphere, or perhaps tingling or temperature change around you in a specific place. Once you have this, assume it is a communicator and begin to describe what you sense and feel about them. How does their presence change you? Describe the essence of the communicator, then describe how the relationship feels to you. Deliver any other evidence that comes to you.

Now move to the message. Offer to the spirit, "What do you want to give? What do you want to talk about?" Follow the lead of the spirit communicator. Pay attention to the inspiration from within. Where does the spirit communicator take you—into the past, to the present, to what has happened since their passing? What impressions can the communicator give you about what is important to them? What does the spirit communicator need to say to their loved one?

Let the experience unfold as you deliver each bit of information. Be sure to involve your sitter's voice along the way, confirming each piece of the message as you go.

When you feel you have delivered everything you can, you can thank the spirit communicator and close. Have your sitter provide feedback about their experience—what made sense and what did not? Use this feedback to better understand your experience.

Take Time for Reflection

How relaxed or easy was the message? Did you find yourself searching? Could your sitter take what was given? If no, was the issue in how you were delivering the information rather than what you were delivering?

15

Troubleshooting Readings

Now that you have everything you need to give a quality mediumship reading, let us explore what to do when our readings don't go the way we hoped. There will be many times when your reading may be less than successful. Realize that this is a natural part of development and mediumship as a whole. Mediumship by its very nature is inconsistent. However, by learning to understand the causes of why our connection feels weak, and how to strengthen it, we can increase our consistency.

In chapter 11 we learned about the triangle of communication between the sitter, the medium, and the spirit communicator. Each of these components must be working properly for a communication to be successful. Therefore, these three areas are an excellent place to discover where the breakdown in our communication is occurring.

Issues Stemming from the Medium

In most instances, the breakdown of a spirit communication can be found with something the medium is doing. This is great news for you since you are the medium and have control over how you respond to whatever issue is arising! In general, issues will arise from tension occurring from desire, distraction, and expectation. By exploring how these causes of tension can manifest, we can then learn what is needed to overcome them.

How to Handle "No"

Handling the dreaded "no" is something that all mediums must learn to do. It can be very hard early on in a medium's development, and even well into it, to experience a no from a sitter. It often leads to tension in the reading and can crash the communication rather quickly. This is because in the beginning of our development, we are often very concerned with the responses of our sitter. This is an example of distraction creating tension. When the medium is too aware of the sitter's reactions, this invites the thinking mind into the process. By refocusing on what we are sensing, we can refocus on our spirit communicator.

Another reason noes can cause issues for a new medium is because developing mediums are insecure about whether they are truly mediumistic or not. Their level of accuracy is usually how they judge this for themselves, which puts pressure on them to achieve or get things right. This ultimately shuts down their energy and then they receive nothing else. The less a medium becomes reactive to a no, the better off they will be. They will be able to maintain the same level of awareness and sense of surrender regardless of how the sitter responds. This is the goal ultimately with getting over a no.

When a sitter does say no—and they will say no—don't freak out. It is just as important for you to get noes in your development as it is for you to get yeses. This is because the noes help you discern between what a yes feels like versus what a no feels like. This way, you start to recognize the specific feeling that accompanies information coming from the spirit versus information originating from your mind. By learning to recognize this feeling through the trial and error of yeses and noes, you develop the ability to discern what information will give you a yes or no before you even say it. Overall, the yeses and noes cultivate your discernment between what is your mind and what is coming from spirit.

It is important to mention that just because you get a no, that doesn't actually indicate that you are wrong. It can be that your sitter is unsure or perhaps hasn't placed the right identity to the communicator in their mind. Also, sitters are notoriously forgetful. The experience of being in a reading can often make a sitter's mind go blank—even forgetting their own mother's name (I have seen this before!). If a piece of information is not taken but you can feel strongly that it is correct, ask the spirit world if they can give it to you in a different way. If that doesn't work, then you can say, "I'm going to put that piece of information aside for now, and if it is important, the spirit will bring it back around." This is true! The spirit will often bring points back up in another way later on in the reading if it is something they want to get across. Sometimes the first way it is delivered is not understood. It is not uncommon to have a sitter email me later after a reading and confirm the part of the reading they had previously said no to, either because they remembered or because they were able to ask someone who knew. If a sitter cannot take a piece of information, do not spend too much time trying to rectify it or figure it out. If after offering this piece of information a couple of different ways it is still not taken, move on from it. Trying to make one piece of information make sense when it is not understood can negatively affect your awareness and focus on your spirit communicator. This will often lead us into our thinking mind. Just accept it for now; if it is important, the spirit will hopefully make sense of it later.

One of the most common reasons why we receive legitimate noes is when we try to interpret the information versus describe what we are getting. As I mentioned in chapter 11, describing what we are experiencing versus interpreting will always lead us to more accurate information. When you get a no, check in with yourself and ask, "Did I deliver this information exactly how I experienced it? What was the stimulus I experienced that made me want to say what I just said?" Then describe that. More often than not, you will find that you gave an interpretation rather than a description.

If you get several noes in a row, that is generally a good indicator that something else is going on in your connection. It may be that your mind is coming into the process. If this happens, take a moment, reset, and bring your awareness back to what you are sensing. We can do this by checking into our heart space or our solar plexus. By doing this, we are taking our focus away from our thinking mind and back to our sense of feeling. Ask yourself, "What am I aware of right now? What can I feel?" and start again.

Ultimately, getting noes is not a big deal. We all will get them working as a medium. They are opportunities to better understand what you are receiving. If you end up getting several noes, it may be that the connection is just not there today. That is okay! I never feel bad or embarrassed if I have to reschedule a reading because it isn't working as well as it normally does. I never want to do less than 100 percent in my readings. If I am not feeling it that day or it isn't landing with the sitter, I will happily say, "I don't think it's working today; can we try again tomorrow?" Each time I have done this, it has almost always worked out perfectly the next time. Just trust that when the moment is right, the reading will work out.

Losing the Link

Another common issue many developing mediums encounter is losing the link. This is when the medium has made a connection, information has begun to flow, and then, at some point in the reading, it feels as though the information has stopped coming or dried up. This is one of the most clear indications that the medium has developed tension in their reading. They have moved into their thinking mind and lost their focus on the spirit presence and what they are feeling.

One reason this can occur is we are reaching for more information rather than waiting for the spirit to bring us something else. Many mediums feel there is a pace the information should be flowing at. When the next thing is not immediately there, they panic and start to reach, or search, for more. This creates tension, which diminishes our ability to sense and feel. If this happens, take a breath and bring your awareness back into the feeling place, the heart space or the solar plexus, and notice what is happening in your awareness at that exact moment. Don't worry about what will come next or if something will be there. Just become sensitive and notice what is happening at that moment. This will generally reconnect you to the spirit presence and bring you back into the communication.

Another reason we lose the link is we become distracted by our sitter's reaction. When our sitter is effusively accepting the information, we will often feel more relaxed and confident in our reading. This makes the connection stronger and easier. However, when our sitter is more reserved or skeptical, it is easy for us to feel tension and our link begins to dry up. The solution to this is the 90/10 rule from chapter 6. Directing our attention to what we are experiencing and lessening our focus on the reaction of our sitter will help us avoid becoming distracted. Also, desire can play a role in creating tension here. The desire to please the sitter or give a strong reading can add tension and pressure to the situation. To counter this, accept that whatever happens in the reading is okay. Whether it works or not, all you can do at this moment is give exactly what you're getting; nothing more. The more we can come at our reading with this mindset, the less we will worry how our sitter responds.

Related to losing the link is the feeling that information is stopping and starting. Almost always this is a sign that the medium is paying too much attention to the information that is coming to them. Their mind is getting involved and trying to understand what it means. The sense of the information starting and stopping is due to the mind's involvement. The medium is switching between being receptive and then trying to "do" something with the information mentally. This breaks the link. You'll often notice when this is occurring in a reading because after each piece of information brought forward, the medium will need a moment to reconnect to the spirit communicator. This is usually marked by a long pause or needing to focus to reconnect.

If you find that this is happening to you, narrate your experience rather than trying to understand it. It is the mind observing the information too much that is breaking the link; therefore, the solution is to just let the information pass through you rather than make sense of it. You can think of this as a train passing through a tunnel carrying the information to the sitter. The first station is the spirit communicator's information or stimulus being loaded on the train. The train should pass straight through the tunnel (the medium) and go directly to its second stop (the sitter). That is two stops. The starting and stopping of the flow of information is due to the medium adding an extra stop in the tunnel—a third stop. They are trying to process or interpret the information and thereby slow it down or completely halt it. This creates an extra step and takes the focus away from the communicator and into the thinking mind. Remember that we should just describe what we are getting as best we can rather than interpret. By doing this, we are removing the third stop in the tunnel and allowing the information to go directly to the sitter. There should only be two stops!

Switching—Is This More Than One Spirit?

Determining whether you have more than one spirit communicator can be a frustrating learning experience for new mediums. This is often experienced as having a communicator bringing information that your sitter can take and then, suddenly, all the information coming forward starts making sense for someone else the sitter knows—yet you did not feel the shift or the change. This can be very frustrating, but it is an important learning experience that will get easier with time and understanding what may be going wrong.

The first reason this can occur is because the medium is not experienced with having more than one communicator. Without experiencing what two spirit presences feel like, sometimes we will not be aware that they are there at all. This is usually coupled with not having a diffused enough energetic awareness when connecting with the spirit. To counter this, keep a relaxed and open awareness by noticing the space in front of you, behind you, on your left and right, and above you. Also, sensing the edges of your aura and noticing everything that's in the space around can help you recognize other spirit presences that may have arrived while you were connecting. These can feel like other densities or pressures in the space around you. If you find that your attention is being drawn to one of these, and you notice that your primary spirit communicator is slowing down or lessening their communication, begin to describe the new communicator just as you would at the beginning of a link. This should help them turn into a fully developed communicator.

The next reason mediums might struggle with a lack of awareness of multiple spirit communicators is not paying enough attention to the power. When a medium is attuned to the power during their reading, the medium will become aware of a shift or a change in the energy, such as an increase or decrease. Oftentimes when a spirit communication is switching to someone else, there will be a slowing down or a dip in the energy before it builds up again. You will also likely notice a buildup in a brand-new area in the energy around you. This is your next communicator. Begin to describe the experience just as you would in the beginning of a link.

Lastly, when the information is vague or not specific enough, this can lead to the sitter beginning to waffle between potential communicators. If I were to say, "This is your husband, his name is John, he died in a plane accident at the age of 65," it is very different from saying, "I have a gentleman here, he feels like family, he died suddenly at an older age and I am seeing the letter J." There is nothing wrong with providing the second example of information, however it is much more direct and clear if we deliver the first example. The second example can leave a sitter confused if this is an uncle, a grandfather, a cousin, or some other relative. The more specific we can be in our information, the easier our sitter will be able to understand it. Of course, you would have to be aware of that level of detail, but the more vague version could be a good starting place to get more detail. As mentioned before, evidence is delivered in layers and as you move through these layers, you could end up with the more specific example.

More likely in small groups or large demonstrations, there are instances where the information that you are getting will be quite specific, you feel a strong link to the spirit, and yet the information is making sense to more than one person. When this occurs, it is often a clear sign that you have more than one communicator. To remedy this, I would suggest offering to the spirit world that they might help you divide up the communicators for you and provide differentiating information. Once you have acknowledged that you have more than one communicator and have asked for separation, the rest of the information should begin to be different from one another.

For example, say I had described the same person and three people could take it. I have two options on how to deal with this. First, I can decide I will read each recipient individually. I might begin with recipient one and bring through information that is different from the other two about them. Then, once I have completed this spirit communication, I would move on to the next sitter and begin again to describe differentiating information about their loved one, followed finally by completing the last communication. In this example, we had similar information that fit three people. Once we recognized that we had more than one, it dovetailed into three unique readings.

Alternatively, you can use this same example, but instead of reading each of the three recipients independently, you can read them all at once. This very example happened to me in a mediumship development workshop. After giving specific and detailed information to narrow down who I was communicating with, I still had three people who could take all the information. I turned to the tutor who was running the class and asked what to do. She said, "Figure it out." So I did. I turned to the three ladies and addressed them one by one: "Your loved one lived by the sea, your loved one lived in the country, and yours lived in the city. Is this correct?" They all validated the information. I then continued, "Your loved one worked in construction, your loved one was a stay-at-home partner, and your loved one was a businessman," which they validated again. I continued working this way until I felt that we had completely differentiated each communicator, and then I offered messages to each sitter from their loved ones and wrapped it all up.

By addressing all three spirit communicators at once, I was able to compare the way that each one felt to one another. It made it quite easy to distinguish because they each had a very different feeling once they were identified as being more than one communicator. Identifying that there is more than one communicator will usually make the rest of the communication feel easier.

When You Get Nothing

One of the greatest sources of anxiety for a developing medium is "What if I get nothing?" This is the fear that your sitter will be there in hopes of getting a message from their loved one and, for whatever reason, nothing comes. Thankfully, this is a very uncommon occurrence, and if it is happening, there's usually a fixable reason.

The first thing I would suggest is to check in with yourself. As we know, tension in our mediumship causes the link to diminish or break. We need to be relaxed and open to become aware of the spirit world. Extreme anxiety, excessive stress, or other strong emotions can cause us to be unable to open our awareness up and thereby cause us to experience nothing. In general, the experience of getting nothing will almost always have to do with some sort of personal issue going on for you in the moment. I have had this experience myself when I have been over worked and stressed. Check in with yourself by asking, "How am I feeling right now? Do I feel any tension or stress? Do I feel anxious or excessively nervous? What is causing these feelings?" If you answer yes to any of these questions, try to discover the root of why this is happening. For example, if I felt excessively nervous, I may ask myself, "Why do I feel nervous?" I may become aware that I am worried that the sitting won't go well because my last reading did not go as well as I would have liked. Once I know what I am worried about, I can counter the source of the tension. In this instance, this fear is sourced in expectation and desire. I am expecting that it may not go well, and I desire that the reading will go well.

To counter this, I need to remember that all I can do is give what is coming to me in the moment. I need to take it one step at a time, one stimulus at a time, and let go of desire for it to work well. The worst that will happen is that I will get a no or that I will have to reschedule the reading. What happens in one reading does not have to mean anything about my abilities as a medium. I will remember that each reading is a brand-new experience, and if I take it one step at a time and follow the lead of the spirit, I am doing my part as the medium.

This kind of self-talk can really make a difference in how we approach our reading. Recognizing the source of the tension and then countering it with the solutions to desire, distraction, and expectations can bring your mindset back to a free, relaxed, and open state. Remember that in mediumship, everything must pass through the medium's mind, so it is important to learn how to maintain our mental and emotional states.

After checking in with mindset, something else to reflect on is whether or not you have been sitting in the power regularly. I know for myself, when I don't sit in the power on a regular basis, my mediumship is not as clear or accurate. Making a link can feel hard or seem distant or even off completely. To remedy this, I try to sit at least four times a week. However, if I have taken a break from working for some time, am feeling particularly disconnected, and know I have a reading coming up, I will start to sit twice a day, fifteen to thirty minutes each time: once in the morning and once at night for the few days leading up to the reading. This helps me to quickly get back into feeling connected.

If after having checked in with yourself, you are free of stress and tension, you have been sitting regularly, and you still are experiencing nothing, it may just not be working that day. It bears repeating that mediumship by its very nature is inconsistent. Therefore, accept this instance as one where it did not work. That is okay. It does not make you any less of a medium; it does not mean you cannot do this work. It was just that moment, for whatever reason. Who knows, maybe the sitter was not meant to receive that message at that time for some reason. Regardless of the reason, the mark of a matured medium is that they can accept when their mediumship is not working and gracefully handle the situation with their sitter. It is much more admirable to say it's not working than try to force it or make it happen. Handle these moments with dignity and honesty, and you will likely have better outcomes.

Sensitive Issues

By the very nature of our work as mediums, we are regularly dealing with sensitive topics. The death of a loved one is one of the most challenging things we will have to experience in our lifetime. The sensitive nature of death can be even further compounded by a tragic or traumatic passing. For developing mediums, topics such as suicide, murder, and miscarriage can sometimes be tricky to navigate.

Dealing with sensitive subjects requires tact and compassion for our sitter. Many times these situations leave our sitter confused and looking for clear answers. It is the job of the medium to provide a safe and supportive environment for the sitter. To this end, we want to be gentle and careful with how we speak about these topics. When dealing with traumatic or sensitive information, it is all in how we convey or deliver the message. Most times students aren't sure what language to use or how to express what they are getting for fear of offending or upsetting the sitter. There are certain phrases that can help prevent this. Instead of saying "this person died by suicide," we can say "this person takes responsibility for their passing." Likewise, with a miscarriage, you could use the phrase "this child did not touch the earth." With topics of murder, you can speak about how the communicator's passing was a result of another person. Using the term "murder" is generally okay, but be mindful of the energy of the sitter.

You do not have to go into great detail when dealing with sensitive topics. By discussing the broader perspective, the sitter can fill in the blanks. It is very likely that they already know the details, and we don't need to make them relive the experience. Our job is to show that the spirit communicator is beyond the state they left this life in. If there are specific questions about the passing the sitter wishes to know, such as a murder, moving closer into the detail may be appropriate, but only at the sitter's request. Most people will not need to know details, and we want to respect that. Moreover, be humble in your attempt to provide answers to these questions. Unless you are certain that the information you are receiving is correct, there is no need to feel obligated to provide further details. If you aren't getting the details, say that. If you are, be certain it is correct before sharing it. Until one is in the more advanced stage of their development, I would refrain from making any strong statements regarding details. Erring on the side of protecting your sitter and accuracy is preferred in these situations.

Other sensitive topics may have less to do with the death of the communicator and more with how they lived their life. Topics such as addiction and abuse can sometimes feel uncomfortable for newer mediums to mention. However, we have to realize that these do happen in people's lives. If someone had a loved one who struggled with addiction their whole life and you make no mention of it, there's a good chance that your sitter will feel you left out a large aspect of their loved one's life. That is not to say that we need to mention it, but more that we need to be open to the multifaceted nature of people. Just because someone was very successful in their life in a business sense does not mean they did not also struggle with addiction or depression. It is okay to mention these topics, but again we need to ensure we use tact and sensitivity. For example, were I aware that someone had experienced some kind of trauma or abuse at the hands of the spirit communicator, I am not going to go into any detail about the trauma. However, I might mention that there was abuse within the relationship and leave it at that. I can then move on to whatever the spirit communicator wishes to say about it, which often is an apology or expressing their remorse. As with any sensitive topic, it is all about how we express it. We want to be gentle without being dramatic or overemphasizing any aspect of it. The medium needs to be mindful of moving to the core of the message—why are they bringing this up?—rather than spending too much time on the traumatic experience.

With any sensitive topic, it is always better to touch upon it lightly without spending too much time there. Remember, these experiences may have been traumatic in the lifetime of the communicator, but these are not their lived experiences anymore. It is important for us to convey this and express how they are now, what emotions or thoughts they wish to convey in hindsight, and any reassurance or making amends for the past. Also, it is okay if the sitter chooses not to accept an apology from a communicator or chooses to hold on to their hurt or resentment. All we can do is deliver the message; what the sitter does with it is up to them. Respect that.

Issues Stemming from the Sitter

Another area where we will likely find a breakdown in the triangle of communication is with our sitter. Sitters come with a lot of different ideas, emotions, and personalities, which can create tension in our readings. The most common source of tension derived from sitters is becoming distracted by them. The way that they react or behave, attitudes they come with, or expectations they have can become a source of distraction for the medium. This is why the best we can do is educate our sitter at the top of our session to let them know what to expect, how you'd like them to respond, and how your mediumship works. You can review chapter 11 on the opening spiel.

Chapter 15

Difficult Sitters

Inevitably, you will come across a difficult sitter. This is someone who comes to the reading as a skeptic, someone looking for one piece of information, or someone who overshares or can't remember details about their loved ones. Again, most of the issues can be avoided by having a clear spiel at the top of the reading. However, let's break these types of sitters down and learn how to work positively with them during the reading.

Skeptical Sitters

Skeptical sitters can be great sitters or very challenging ones depending on the type of skeptic that they are. There is a spectrum of skeptical sitters, with an open-minded skeptic on one end and a closed-minded skeptic on the other. An open-minded skeptic is actually an ideal sitter because they are open to engaging the process, willing to enter into the experience the medium is having, but will also approach the entire reading with a sense of curiosity and careful consideration. This sense of openness combined with thoughtful scrutiny creates a sitter who won't accept just anything unless it is accurate. They are genuinely curious to find out if mediumship is real or not. Reading for an open-minded skeptic is also fun because they are genuinely surprised and pleased by the discovery that this work is real.

On the other end of the spectrum are the closed-minded skeptics. These are the people who are not worth reading for at all. A closed-minded skeptic is someone who, no matter what evidence is brought forward, will look to discredit and dismiss it as incorrect or invalid. Their entire aim is to prove that this work is not real because their mind is already made up. Thankfully, a hard-nosed, closed-minded skeptic will not generally find their way into your reading room. If they do, it is usually because someone has purchased the reading for them.

Most skeptical people will fall somewhere closer to the open-minded skeptic, which is a lovely read. Should you find yourself reading a skeptic that is closer to the closed-minded skeptic on the scale, there are some things you can do to help remedy the situation to the best of your ability.

First, you will want to explain as much as possible at the top of the reading about what to expect and how it works. Explaining how mediumship works will be so important because a skeptic comes to readings with a preconceived idea of how it should work. In particular, they tend to associate it with what they have seen on TV or assume that it's cold or hot reading. They will likely not give a whole lot in their responses, can feel closed off, and can be less willing to engage the process. Explaining to a skeptic how setting aside their preconceived ideas and relaxing will produce better results can help the situation. Even expressing how you might have been a skeptic too had it not been for your personal experiences can sometimes help. Offer to answer any questions they might have to help put them at ease.

Next, decide that you are not going to let their reactions and behaviors affect you. Instead, you are going to tune into the compassionate part of yourself and where this place within you relates to this place in them. Trying to find a common energetic connection as you're attuning can be very helpful.

As you enter the communication, do your best to trust yourself and your reading. By the time you will be working with the public, you will have spent years of development and will have cultivated an understanding of how you work. Trust your connection and your flow. Especially in this instance, you must trust the spirit and take it one impression at a time. Your sitter may not be very helpful in this time period, so if you aren't getting yeses right away and more maybes and I'm not sures, trust that as you continue to connect, more will come. Continue to focus on relaxing and getting to know your spirit communicator.

If your sitter begins to test you or ask you questions before you've said they could, just gently remind them of the rules you established at the top. Since you will have already let them know how you work, do your best to remain kind but firm with your boundaries. You do not have to prove anything to anyone. All you need to do is trust what you're getting. If the reading ends with your sitter remaining an unbeliever, that is okay. Your job is not to convince anyone; your job is to relay your experience.

If you find that the sitter is too challenging, causes you to get too much in your head, or you are uncomfortable with proceeding with the reading, it is completely within your right to end the session at any time. What we do is a service, and it should be respected and valued. If you feel that this is not happening in your sitting, you should end your session. You can respectfully express why you are ending your session or simply say that this is not the right fit at this time.

Do your best with skeptics as they too are looking for answers (most of the time). We want to offer our services to everyone who will meet us with respect and consideration. For those who can, they get the opportunity to have their worldview shifted in a very beautiful way.

Sitters Who Want Something Specific

You will have sitters who will come to you with an agenda. Most of the time, sitters will have someone specific that they wish to hear from. This is not a problem. However, they should be informed at the top of the reading that mediums cannot guarantee to bring through the loved one they're hoping for, but that you will do your best. You should also mention that sometimes, a different spirit communicator might come forward first before the person they were hoping for. Very likely, the next spirit communicator will be who they were wishing to hear from. Having them primed with the knowledge that just because the first communicator is not who they were hoping for doesn't mean they won't come through. You can also reassure them that after the second communicator, if the spirit person they were hoping to hear from doesn't come through, you can then ask them who they were hoping to hear from and you will see if you can make that link for them. In my experience, nearly every time I give a reading, thanks to the intelligence of the spirit, the person the sitter was hoping to speak to comes in the first or second communication.

Sometimes the sitter can bring their own tension to the session. We sometimes want to hear from a loved one so badly that we are very constricted in our energy, which can make a clear communication extra challenging. If the spirit person they were hoping to hear from does not come through, this may be part of the reason why. It may be that this wasn't the right connection or moment for this communication. Remember that a communication is a three-way connection, and all parts must be working well for a successful link. While it is very rare that a hoped-for loved one doesn't come through, it does happen. Don't beat yourself up if you didn't make the connection or link. Just do your best and forget the rest.

You will also come across sitters who may get who they wish to hear from in the first spirit communication, but they are there for a very specific piece of information. This can sometimes be a code word or perhaps a name. Very often these kinds of sitters can bring a lot of tension and angst with them because they won't fully allow themselves to enter into the communication without this code word or piece of evidence first. You can be giving them all kinds of accurate information, but they are so fixated on this one piece that they disregard the rest of the reading. With these sitters, explaining how a communication unfolds and that more detailed information develops in a reading can help ease some of the tension. Be aware of any tension in your reading caused by feeling obligated to try and get the specific piece of evidence they are hoping for. Remember that you do not have to prove anything to anyone. Just give what is coming to you; that is all you can do. Hopefully, through the intelligence of the spirit, they can bring through whatever the sitter needs, which may or may not include this special piece of information. But also realize anything is possible and trust the spirit; they may very well bring this. The key is don't try to go after it. Focus on keeping your connection relaxed and strong. Let the excellent evidence be a byproduct of your surrendered state to the spirit.

Issues Stemming from the Spirit Communicator

I chose to include this section not because issues truly do stem from the communicator, but rather our experience of these issues seems that way. I often hear new mediumship students say, "This communicator doesn't want to talk" or "This spirit is holding back" or "The spirit just left." This has not been my experience. If a spirit person shows up, it is because they want to communicate; otherwise, why would they be there? More often the issue arises in the way the medium is interpreting how the spirit person is communicating.

For example, a spirit person shows up and they are not bringing a lot of information; they are standing back a bit and just observing. Some students might mistakenly interpret this as the spirit not wanting to communicate. However, most of the time this is evidential information. Instead of assuming that the communicator doesn't want to speak, describe the behavior you see or sense they are doing. Almost always this will be understood by the communicator as a way that they behaved. Moreover, usually after that piece of information is accepted, the communicator becomes much clearer and stronger. This is because they were intentionally impressing you with a reserved, pulled-back quality. It's easier for the new medium to misinterpret this as not communicating because that's what it feels like. But just like very boisterous and strong spirit communicators who come in full force intensely, these communicators are coming in showing how they were in life.

———

Remember that it is always better to describe your experience rather than try to interpret it. The best we can do in any reading is to just notice, describe, and let it go. It is not our job to interpret or understand the information coming through. Sometimes we will understand its meaning and context; other times we won't. That's okay. Just give your experience and let go of an attachment to the outcome. Remember that your job as the medium is to get out of the way. Also, the more we can manage expectations of our sitter by explaining things thoroughly at the top of the reading and answering any questions, the better we can avoid many of the issues discussed in this chapter. With anything that arises, trust the spirit and trust yourself. Things will not always go as planned, but if we can meet them with flexibility, compassion, and respect, they can be managed and have a better outcome.

Conclusion

Mediumship Beyond the Message

Through this journey we have taken together, we have accomplished so much. We have dispelled myths about the spirit world. We have explored how we can learn to quiet and still our awareness and how we can sense and feel the energy around us. We have learned to describe our experiences and better understand people, essence, evidence, and the message. Our journey has shown us what is possible when we allow the spirit world to lead us and provide real, tangible evidence of their reality. My hope is that you were able to begin to touch the spirit world and gain a solid foundation as to what underpins all of mediumistic and psychic awareness. Through this tool kit, you are now equipped to move forward with your development. But what comes now? What comes after the knowledge that we can deliver a message from those in spirit? Where does our development go from here?

To begin with, I think that development never ends. We are constantly growing and maturing our mediumship and connection to the spirit world. I know for myself, I still sit regularly for my development of my mediumship because there is no limit to what the spirit can accomplish with continued dedication. The bar is very high for me as to what constitutes quality mediumship, and I want to make sure that I end up being a medium who upholds this standard. In this way, our development is never finished until we make our crossing to the other side and join our guides, family, and friends.

But much more than just being able to pass a quality message for those on the physical side of life, there is so much more to one's mediumistic awareness that needs to be explored. What I have provided for you here is a tool set through which you can begin to understand your own spiritual nature and how you fit into this bigger scheme of life. As my mentor Eileen Davies has always taught us, "Mediumship leads you to the threshold of your own inner being." These wise words are precisely what I wish for you to understand as you continue on your mediumistic development journey. You now have access to a way of experiencing the world and reality that is much more subtle, finer, and adds a depth and richness that perhaps you previously were unaware of. There is a whole world of experiences to explore beyond just passing messages along. Cultivating your psychic sensitivity, working with other forms of mediumship, and maybe even developing your own ways of working with spirit are all possibilities to be had as you move forward.

With that said, it is important for you to understand that reading a book and trying a few exercises does not make you a developed medium. I have shared with you the tools that I know and understand, but it is through years of dedicated work and development that you come to understand your spiritual abilities. This will require you to participate in a spiritual circle of some sort, whether a home circle where you sit in the power or one led by an experienced, respected, and trusted teacher on this topic. Nothing can replace the work you do sitting in the power and sitting in a development circle consistently over time.

There is a difference between knowledge and wisdom. Knowledge is what you have gained from this book. Wisdom is the application of this knowledge over time, matured through experience. We want to be wise mediums, not just knowledgeable ones. Once you have spent a sufficient amount of time in your development circle and you have faced every obstacle, insecurity, and challenge that can arise in a sitting, then you may begin to work with the public. As I have emphasized over and over in this book, we want to be sure that we have cultivated ourselves in such a way that we are prepared to handle the delicate task of helping those in the incredibly vulnerable state of grief. Not only that, what is often lost on new mediums is the wisdom gained that can only come through time and experience. No book, teacher, or mentor could ever teach you these specific lessons that only time can show you. This is because your understanding of the subject matures as you mature. There is no race to the finish line or arrival point. Take your time with your mediumship and you will be rewarded with quality, consistent, and reputable work.

A large part of the journey in mediumship is learning to get out of the way. This is a practice that takes years and years of development. It is a constant skill to cultivate as our mind is very desirous to engage in all of the things you do. A quality medium learns how to remove themselves from their work. In this way, they make more and more room for the spirit world—rather than their own wants and desires—to come through. This takes time. What is often realized as you move along your journey is when you think you have let go and surrendered, it isn't until you have surrendered even more deeply that you recognize how much you were still holding on before. Recognize that on this path, you will often be faced with realizations that you don't know what you don't know until you do. How's that for cryptic? However, those of you who read this and have been on this journey for a long time will recognize its meaning and value.

Ultimately, I feel that the greatest growth in our mediumship comes when we surrender what we want out of our mediumship and instead say to spirit, "Lead thou me on, keep thou my feet, I do not ask to see the distant scene, one step enough for me." This line from the hymn "Lead, Kindly Light"[15] has always touched me deeply. It is this state of full surrender of the path of your spiritual unfoldment that has always landed me exactly where I needed to be—both to help others and find

15   John Henry Newman, Geraldine Farrar, Walter B. Rogers, and John Bacchus Dykes (1916), https://www.loc.gov/item/jukebox-17864/.

great success in my work. I have been led to the most amazing teachers and mentors, incredible experiences of true spiritual phenomenon, beautiful moments of healing and growth, amazing examples of the power and reality of spirit, and opportunities that worked out better than I ever would have hoped or planned. All of this comes from the mindset of "one step enough for me."

And so I pass along this message that was given to me by those wiser before me: "Your gift will take you where you're meant to be." If you can meet the spirit world with open palms and reach out to the spiritual side of life, they will always reach back down and meet you there. Let your work be recognized not by the fame, the fortune, or the attention you may get from your skill, but rather by the hearts that you touch, the love that you share, and the example that you are in the world to others. Cultivate patience, compassion, and love first, because this is the gift that is needed far more than another medium or psychic. Spiritualize yourself, and the gifts that come along with that will be but a footnote in the grand scheme of your experiences.

Thank you for reading my book. I hope you found it helpful, and I hope you grow to be even more of the beautiful soul that you are.

x Michael

Recommended Resources

Meditations

https://www.mediummichaelmayo.com/shop

Books

Austen, A. W., ed. *Teachings of Silver Birch*. Melbourne, Victoria: Vision Australia Information Library Service, 2004.

Cattenach, Rosalind. *'Best' of Both Worlds: A Tribute to a Great Medium*. England: Saturday Night Press Publications, 2016.

Chapman, George. *Surgeon from Another World*. London: W. H. Allen, 1978.

Garrett, Eileen J. *Awareness*. New York: Creative Age Press, 1945.

———. *Many Voices: The Autobiography of a Medium*. New York: Putnam, 1968.

Harris, Louie. *Alec Harris: The Full Story of His Remarkable Physical Mediumship*. York, England: Saturday Night Press, 2009.

Leonard, Gladys Osborne. *My Life in Two Worlds*. London: Cassell & Co., 1992.

Parnia, Sam. *Erasing Death: The Science That Is Rewriting the Boundaries between Life and Death*. New York: HarperOne, 2014.

Smith, Gordon. *Beyond Reasonable Doubt: The Case for Supernatural Phenomena in the Modern World*. London: Coronet, 2019.

———. *The Unbelievable Truth: A Medium's Guide to the Spirit World*. Carlsbad, CA: Hay House, 2004.

Upton, Bernard, and Jane Helen Hughes. *The Mediumship of Helen Hughes*. London: Spiritualist Press, 1946.

Van Praagh, James. *Healing Grief: Reclaiming Life after Any Loss*. London: Piatkus, 2009.

———. *Talking to Heaven: A Medium's Message of Life after Death*. London: Piatkus, 2009.

Websites

https://www.Oakbridgeinstitute.org

https://www.Mediummichaelmayo.com

https://www.thescoleexperiment.com

https://www.Leslieflint.com

https://www.Cidadedaluz.com.br

https://www.Windbridge.org

To Write to the Author

If you wish to contact the author or would like more information about this book, please write to the author in care of Llewellyn Worldwide and we will forward your request. Both the author and the publisher appreciate hearing from you and learning of your enjoyment of this book and how it has helped you. Llewellyn Worldwide cannot guarantee that every letter written to the author can be answered, but all will be forwarded. Please write to:

Michael Mayo
℅ Llewellyn Worldwide
2143 Wooddale Drive
Woodbury, MN 55125-2989

Please enclose a self-addressed stamped envelope for reply
or $1.00 to cover costs. If outside the USA, enclose
an international postal reply coupon.

Many of Llewellyn's authors have websites with additional information and resources. For more information, please visit our website:

WWW.LLEWELLYN.COM